Metal Techniques of Bronze Age Masters:

All Chained Up

Victoria Lansford

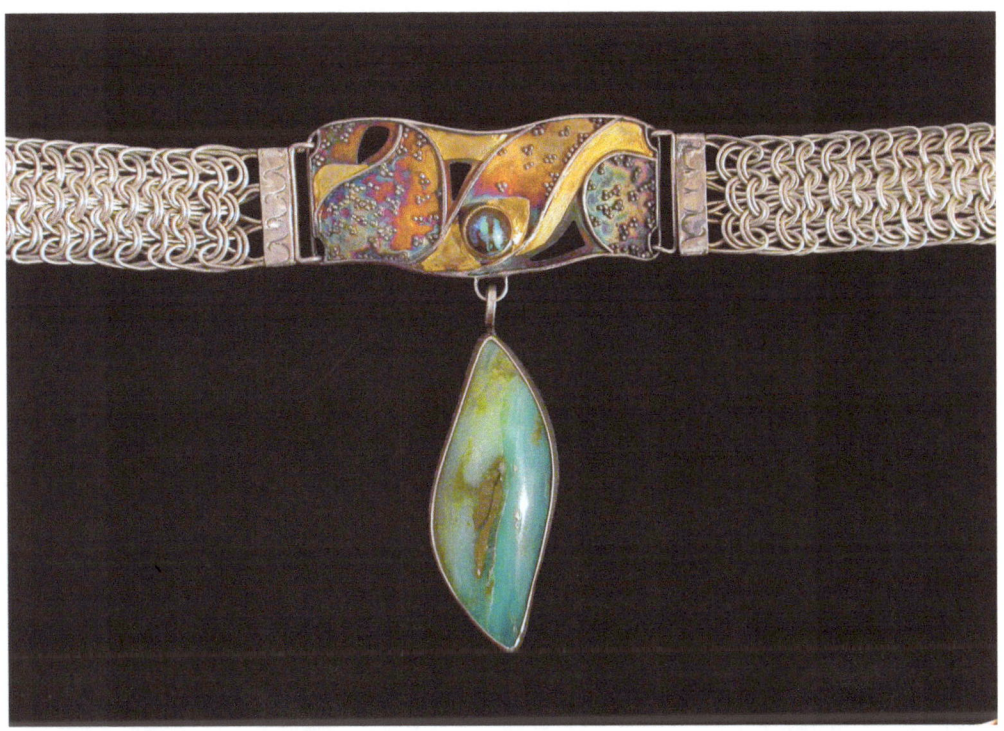

Spiral Publications

Atlanta, Georgia

Published by
Spiral Publications
Atlanta, Georgia
www.spiralpublications.com

Printed in the United States of America

ISBN 978 0 9821833 1 1

Front cover artwork:
Victoria Lansford, *Landscape of My Dreams,* Side Weave Mesh pattern bracelet with a clasp of high relief Eastern repoussé from straight grain mokume gane; 18k, 22k gold, fine silver, sterling silver, copper, Koroit opal; 7" long x 1-5/8" wide 2007
Entwine, Russian filigree pendant on a 2-Directional Double-Weave chain; 22k gold, sterling silver, fine silver, chrysocolla drusy; pendant 3" long, 16" chain; 2007
Vertebracelet, a series of Vertebrate pattern bracelets with Russian filigree, reticulation or granulation clasps; sterling silver, fine silver, 22k gold, Koroit opal 7-1/4" long x 7/8" wide; 2008

Back cover:
Rivers of Gold V, granulation, kum boo, and Side Weave Mesh choker 22K, 24K gold, sterling silver, fine silver, Peruvian opal; 2006 (also page 1)
Rivers of Gold VI, granulation, kum boo, and Side Weave Mesh bracelet; sterling silver, fine silver, 24K gold, Peruvian opal; 2006
Vertebracelet, a series of Vertebrate pattern bracelets with Russian filigree, reticulation or granulation clasps; sterling & fine silver, 18k, 22k gold, Koroit opal 7-1/2" long x 3/4" wide; 2006

Page 3: *Glimmer,* Russian filigree amulet on a 1-Direction Single-Weave chain, 18k, 22k, 24k gold, sterling & fine silver, Koroit opal; 2004

Other titles in the series,

Metal Techniques of
Bronze Age Masters:

Russian Filigree (DVD)

Rings (DVD)

For information on ordering,
please visit
www.victorialansford.com

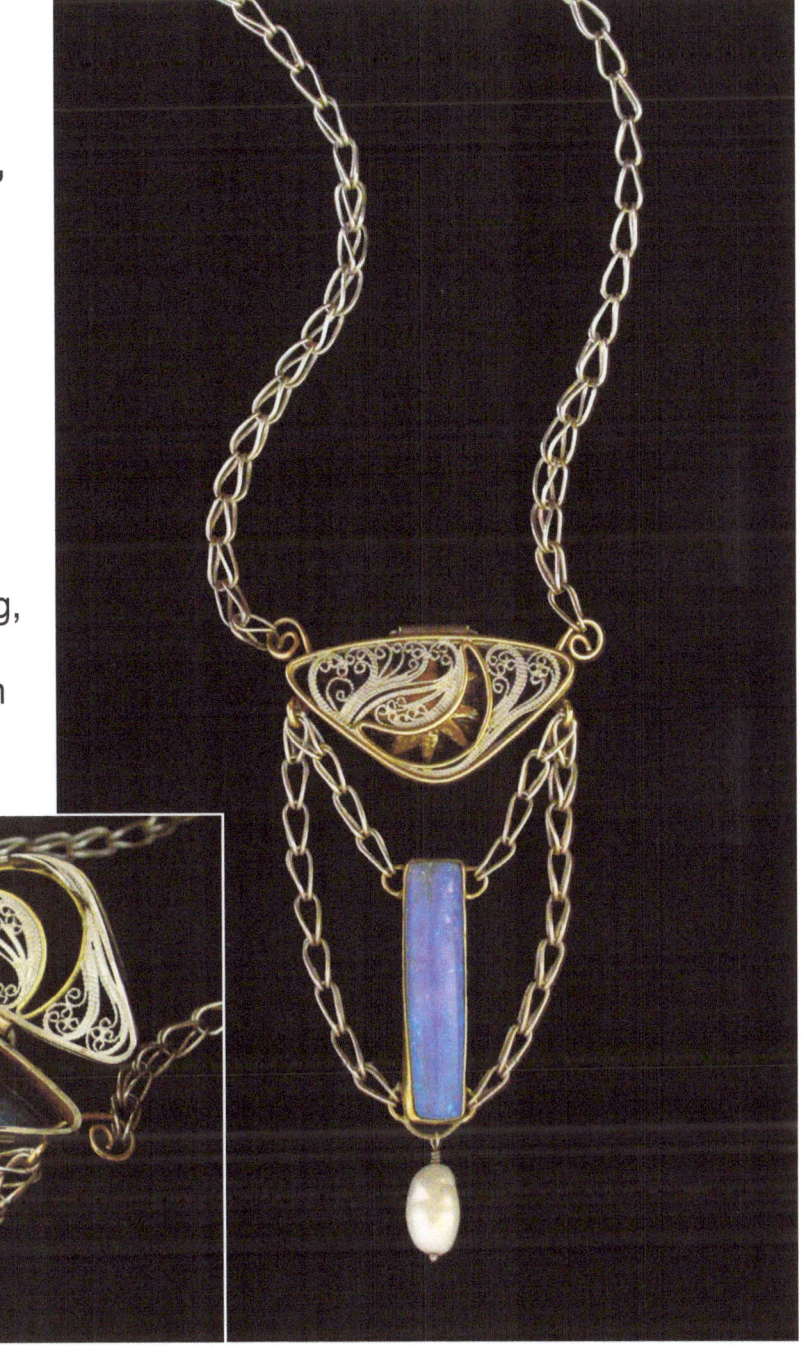

To Chris - Forever linked

Contents

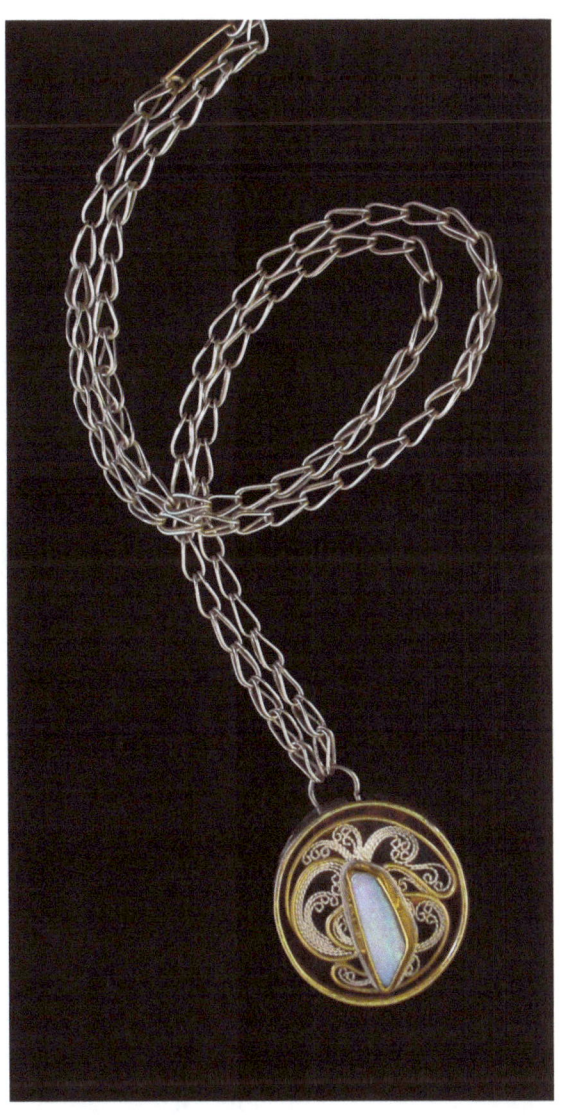

Russian filigree, chased, and wire granulation spinning pendant on a 1-Direction Single-Weave chain, 18k Gold, 22k gold, sterling silver, fine silver, Koroit opal; 1-1/2" in diameter, 22" chain; 2004

Introduction

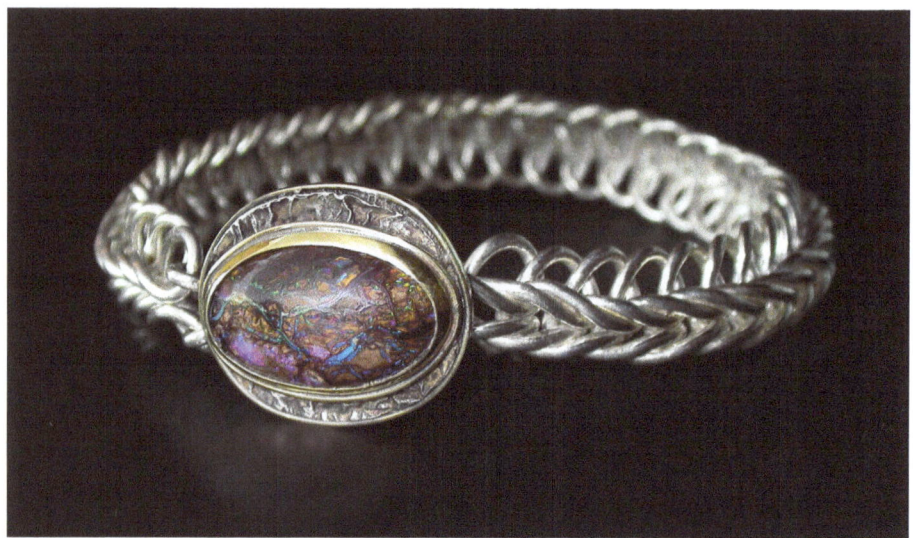

Vertebracelet

a series of Vertebrate pattern bracelets with Russian filigree, reticulation or granulation clasps; sterling & fine silver, 18k, 22k gold, Koroit opal 7-1/2" long x 3/4" wide; 2006

opposite: Rivers of Gold IV

Side weave mesh pattern bracelet with granulation and kum boo clasp; Sterling & fine silver, 22k, 24k gold, Koroit opal; 7" long x 1" wide; 2006

When I first began selling my work in 1989, I marketed it as completely handwrought and one-of-a-kind, but when I looked at the manufactured chains I was adding to my pieces, I realized that I was not being true to my vision. Since I was quite happy in the land of details and tiny wires, I began investigating my chain-making options. I've always preferred chains that have links closed by heat or by cold connections that can't be seen. Most of all I hate cleaning up misplaced lumps of solder.

All of these considerations led me to explore fused chains in the style of ancient Mediterranean and Near Eastern cultures. Interestingly, the Romans get credit for loop in loop chains, which are often called "Roman Chains," though the ancient Egyptians, Sumerians, and Etruscans made loop in loop chains first, soon followed by the Greeks. One can hardly look at the jewelry of those cultures without encountering what I call the 1-Direction Single-Weave or the 2-Directional Double-weave loop in loop chain.

Before these early metalsmiths soldered, they fused. The technique of soldering, using alloys that melt at a lower temperature to join together two pieces of metal that melt at a higher temperature, was an *ah-ha* moment that came second. It was a big technological leap and a huge advantage for fabrication, but I'm betting these ancient smiths had the process of fusing so perfected that the addition of solder wasn't such an advantage for techniques like granulation and chain-making. It's relatively easy enough to control the heat on small pieces, and while a soldered joint is stronger because metal has been added to the seam, fused joints of fine silver or high karat gold are nearly invisible and quite flexible, yet strong enough to be formed and woven.

"These Are a Few of My Favorite" Chains

I confess that what prompted me to begin creating one-of-a-kind works of art was that I hate repetitive tasks. Chain-making, however, is the exception. There is something zen-like about the process of forming, fusing, and weaving links. I find it to be a kind of meditation in action and work that I look forward to doing.

Over the years I've developed a few favorite styles of loop in loop chains and used them more than any other types of chains. From making so many I've found ways to speed up and assembly line the process. My preference is for chains that appear braided or have herringbone pattern to the weave, so starting in 1997 I became somewhat obsessed with how to create such patterns for wider as well as mesh chains.

Through much experimentation, I have invented new patterns of fused chains, based on ancient techniques. It's my privilege now to be able to share my methods with you, which I hope you will use in your own original designs. Please experiment with the gauges of wire, link sizes, styles, and variations of these chains, and feel free to send pictures! My email is victoria@victorialansford.com.

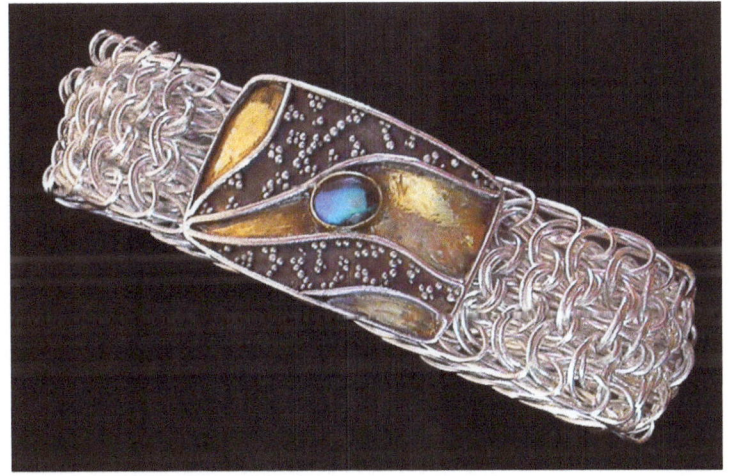

Studio Safety

The instructions in this book are for people, who are familiar with how to operate a torch and possess other basic metalsmithing skills. Always use common sense in the studio. Keep loose clothing and hair back and away from torches and machinery. Use safety glasses and particle masks when using the flex shaft. Keep gas tanks chained to a workbench or other heavy support. Use adequate ventilation when working with chemicals. The best kind of exhaust system is one that pulls fumes away from you rather than an overhead system, which pulls fumes past your face.

Things to keep handy
- A fire extinguisher
- Baking Soda
- A container of water
- Your awareness at all times!

Keep your fire extinguisher where you can easily grab it in case of emergency. For instance, don't put it on the far side of your soldering station, where you might have to reach past something on fire to

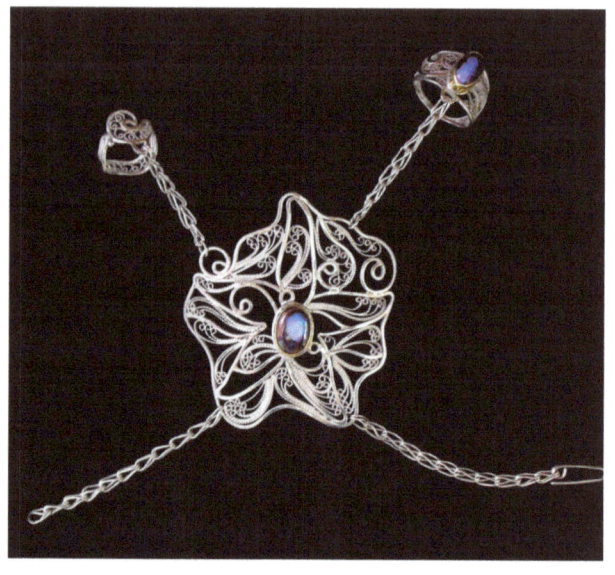

Scheherazade

Russian filigree handpiece and rings connected with 1-Direction Single-Weave chains; Sterling & fine silver, 22k gold, Koroit opals; 3" long x 3" wide; 2004

grab it. Fire extinguishers have expirations dates and pressure regulators. Make sure to check yours! Paper towels or sketch paper lying around is a potential hazard, so keep your soldering area clear of those or other flammables. To protect your fingers, always polish chains on a flex shaft or by hand. **Never polish chains on a polishing machine!!!**

Tools & Materials

German charcoal block (3-4 are ideal)

Joyce Chen™ kitchen shears

Round and flat pliers

Long fine chain nose pliers

Flat nylon pliers

"Bracelet Bending" nylon pliers

Oblique or end cutters

Air/acetylene torch with #3 tip
  (other torch types may not fuse heavier gauges of wire)

Tweezers

Scriber

Flex shaft

Mini muslin polishing buff for the flex shaft

Screw top mandrels for the flex shaft

Blue rouge polishing compound

SparkleSparkle Ultracloth™ polishing cloth

Double stick tape

Cardstock

Dowels, dapping punches, or other round mandrels in 11, 13, & 19mm diameters.

Metal ruler or calipers

20 gauge, solder filled sterling jump rings

16, 20 and 22 gauge fine silver round wire

6" of 12 gauge 1/2 round sterling wire

12" of 18 gauge square or round sterling wire

Beads, pearls, or other dangles

Sheet silver, pickle, paste flux, and solder for clasps for the Side Weave Mesh and Vertebrate patterns

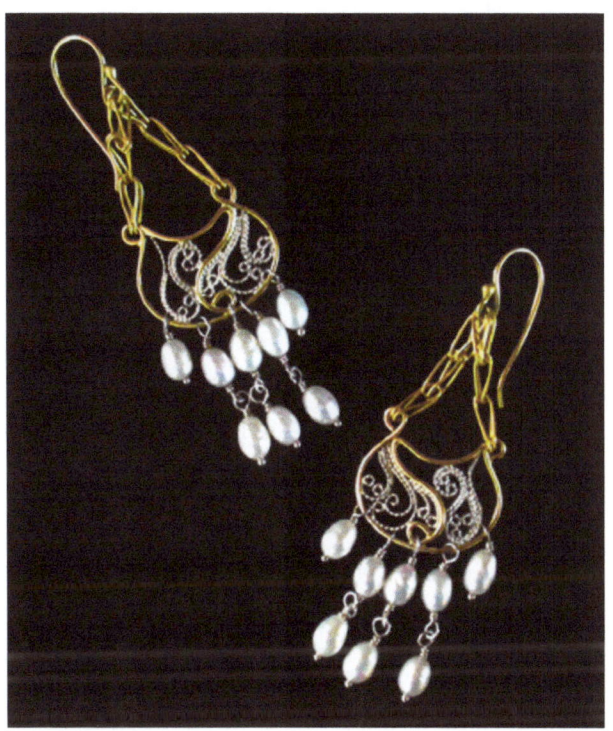

Minuet

Russian filigree and 1-Direction Single-Weave chain
earrings; 18k, 22k gold, fine silver, Biwa pearls
1-3/4" x 3/4"; 2003

Metals

Working with Silver

There are several different ways to create ancient pattern loop in loop chains. Some people use sterling silver and solder the links. Some people fuse the links in a kiln with the aid of a torch. I prefer to use fine silver not only because fused joints leave no clean up, but also because the joints are flexible enough to allow them to be shaped in a myriad of ways. It is possible to fuse sterling (the style of granulation I do is with sterling silver and 18k gold), but the joints are inherently brittle and will pop when forming chain links. To fuse links from 24 guage and larger metal, using a kiln slows down the process because it takes more time to lay out the links on the tiny kiln surface. For fusing 26 gauge and smaller links, it may help prevent so many links from melting accidentally.

Working with Gold

When making gold chains, I most often use 22k gold. Most metal fabricators alloy 22k with fine silver and very little copper, which makes it work well for fused chains. For 18k or lower, it is best to alloy it yourself, so that you know the metals used and their proportions. More than a tiny bit of copper, or any other metals besides fine silver in the mix, will cause very brittle joints, which will snap open when you form the links.

Another suggestion when working with gold is to use one gauge smaller wire than you would if you were making the same chain in fine silver. Because of its yellow color, gold is less reflective than silver, so a chain in 18k or 22k gold will appear larger and denser than the same exact size chain in fine silver. For example, if I would use 22 gauge fine silver with a 9.5mm mandrel, then I would use 24 gauge 22k gold with the same size mandrel to create a chain of the same apparent delicacy.

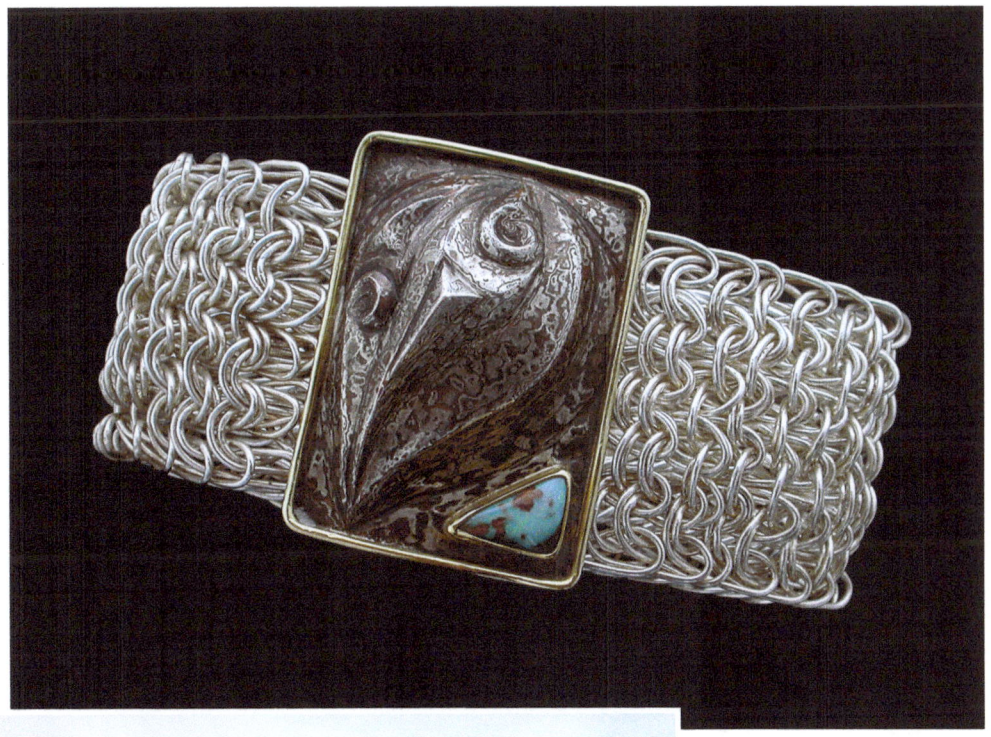

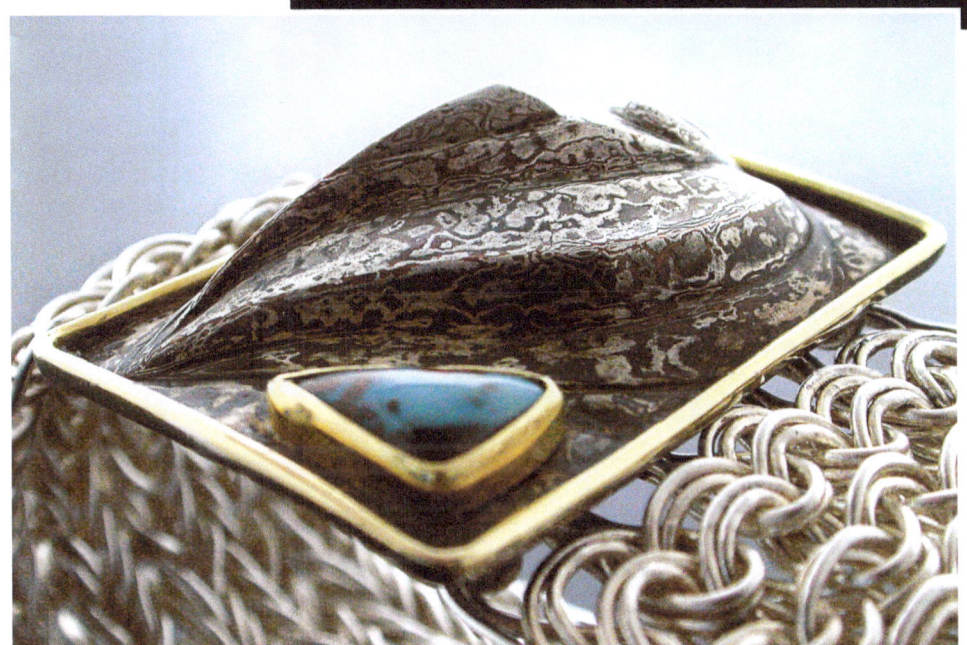

Landscape of My Dreams

Side Weave Mesh pattern bracelet with a clasp of high relief Eastern repoussé from straight grain mokume gane; 18k, 22k gold, fine silver, sterling silver, copper, Koroit opal
7" long x 1-5/8" wide
2007

The Basics of Fusing Links

The process for fusing links is the same for all of the chains in this book. Specific wire gauge sizes and mandrel diameters are given at the beginning of each pattern.
To start the most basic pattern, the 1-Direction Single-weave, you will need .5 troy ounce of fine silver round wire and a 10 or 11mm mandrel.

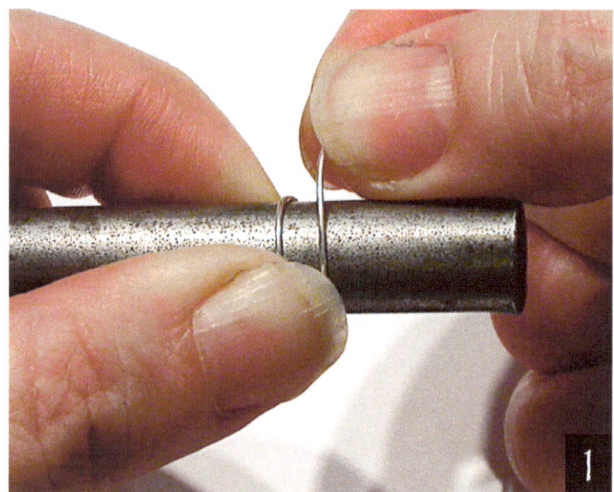

1-2 Wrap the fine silver round wire around the appropriate size mandrel to form a coil. It does not need to be pulled tight, but leaving very little space between wraps will keep the links uniform in size.

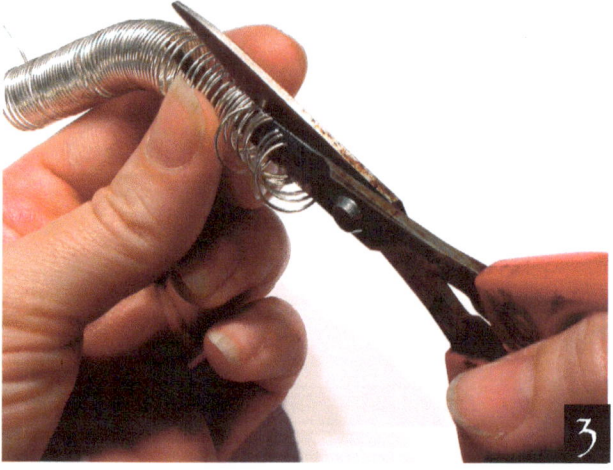

3 Cut the coil with Joyce Chen™ scissors

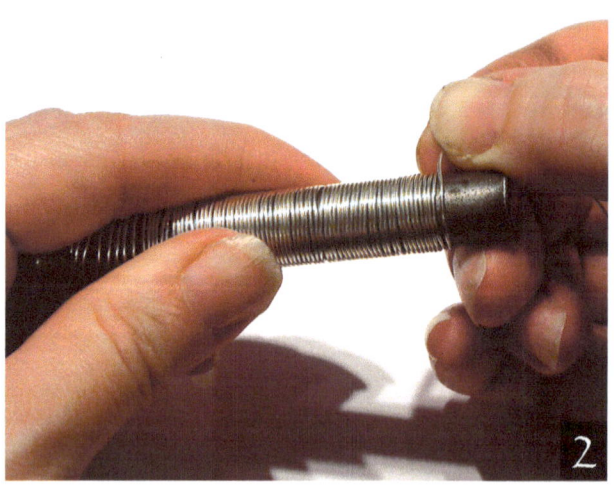

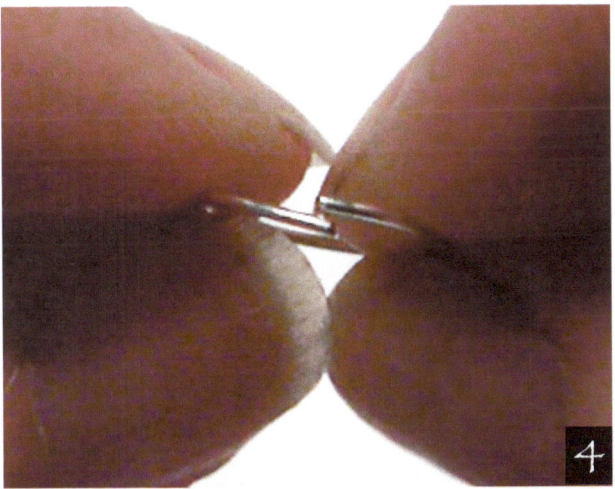

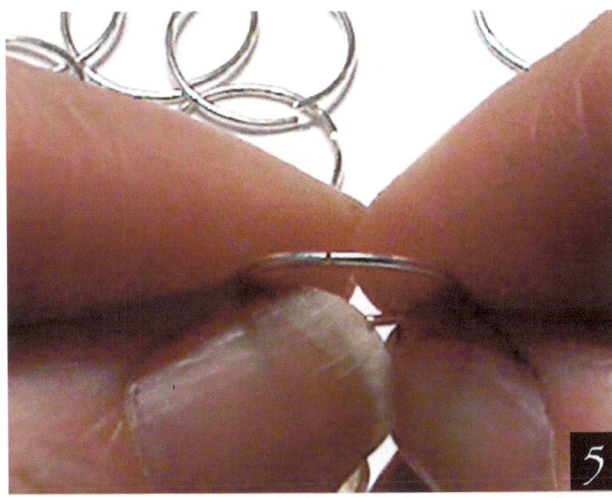

Speed Things Up!

The first time you fuse links, lay them directly onto a charcoal block and see how it goes. After you get the hang of fusing, assembly lining the process of closing and laying out links can really save time.

Place rows of double stick tape on pieces of card stock. (I use cut up manilla file folders.) Pat your hands on a charcoal block and then pat them on the taped cards. The charcoal dust will leave the tape slightly tacky but not as sticky. Lay the closed links with the seams facing away from you.

Turn the card around so that the seams face you. Gently transfer the

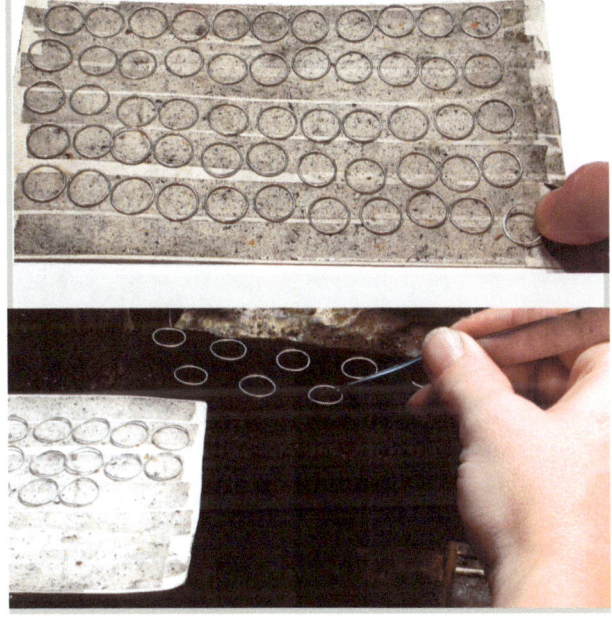

4-5 Close the scam of each link by over crossing the ends, over crossing them the other way, and then pulling them back to meet with tension and no space in between.

Remember: links that aren't closed well, wont fuse well!

links to the charcoal block with tweezers. (If they pull open when you lift them, the tape is too sticky.) Line up the links in 3 or 4 staggered rows on the charcoal blocks **with the seams facing you.**

Fill several cards with closed links, and stack them in a tight fitting box that will keep them from sliding around. This way you can close links away from the studio or even while watching TV and have them ready for fusing. This is also a big time saver if you do not yet have a studio of your own.

Using 3-4 charcoal blocks further speeds up the assembly line process.

Correct Torch Position

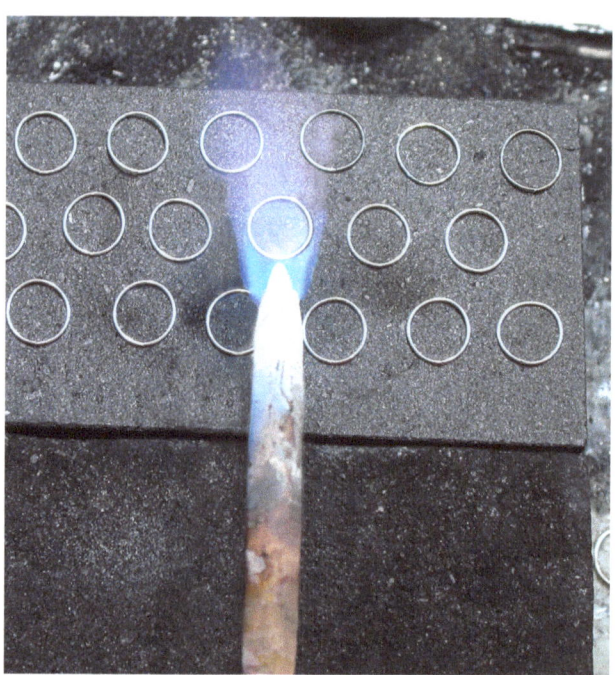

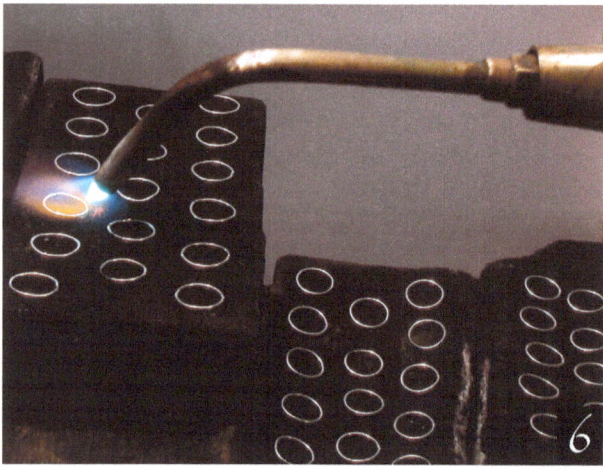

6 Start with the first link on the back row and heat opposite the seam for a 3-5 seconds. The link will need to be hot all over to fuse at the seam. Also, heating opposite the seam expands the metal across the back, forcing the seam closed

Watch Out!!!

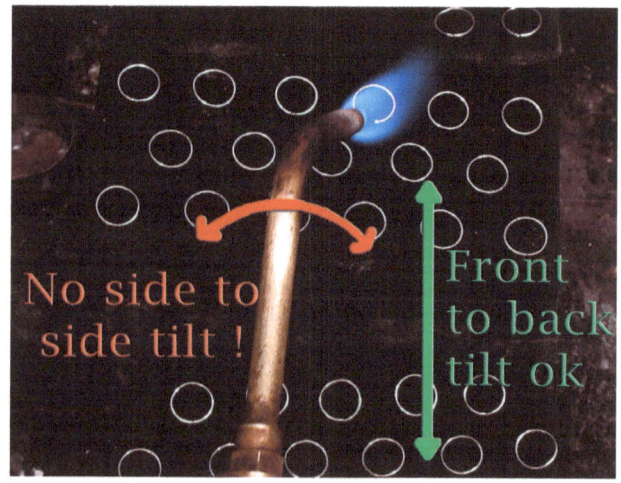

No side to side tilt !

Front to back tilt ok

The Fused, the Melted, and the Bumpy

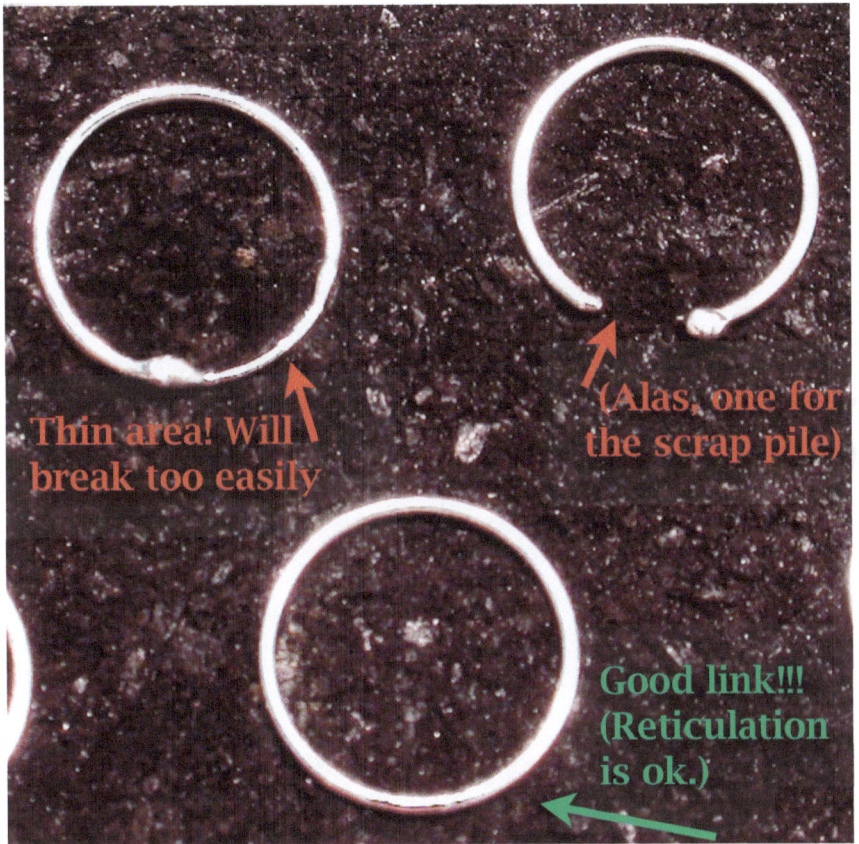

Thin area! Will break too easily

(Alas, one for the scrap pile)

Good link!!! (Reticulation is ok.)

Melting Links?

Your torch may be too high. If turning it down doesn't help, change your torch tip to a smaller size.

Watch out that your torch isn't tilted side to side.

Make sure that the link is completely closed and laying flat on the block.

Not Fusing?

Heat the back of the link for longer before moving down to heat the seam.

Make sure that your flame is pointing at the seam and not at the space inside the link.

Links that did not fuse the first time can be fused the next time.

and keeping it from popping open. Once the link is heated, move the hot point of the flame (just past the blue cone) to point at the seam. The metal around the seam will "mirror" like flowing solder. When you see the seam flow together remove the torch immediately!

The fused area may have some slight reticulation (rough surface), which is fine and won't be visible (bottom link in photo), but links that have blobs or obviously thick/thin areas are not useable because they will be too weak and will break (top left link).

Ok, so by now you may have discovered the links don't all turn out perfectly. When learning this process, if you get 50% of your links fused correctly, you're doing quite well. Trust me: you will improve with practice! Fusing links takes a little patience but weaving them is much faster and a lot of fun.

Fusing Gold Links

The process of fusing gold links is the same as for silver except for the placement of the links on the charcoal block. Place the links around the edge of the block with the seams just barely hanging off. Heat opposite the seam (gold does not have to be heated all over to fuse, but heating the back will prevent the seam from expanding and popping open) and then aim the torch perpendicular to the seam to fuse. For more information on working with gold, see page 10 in the Metals chapter.

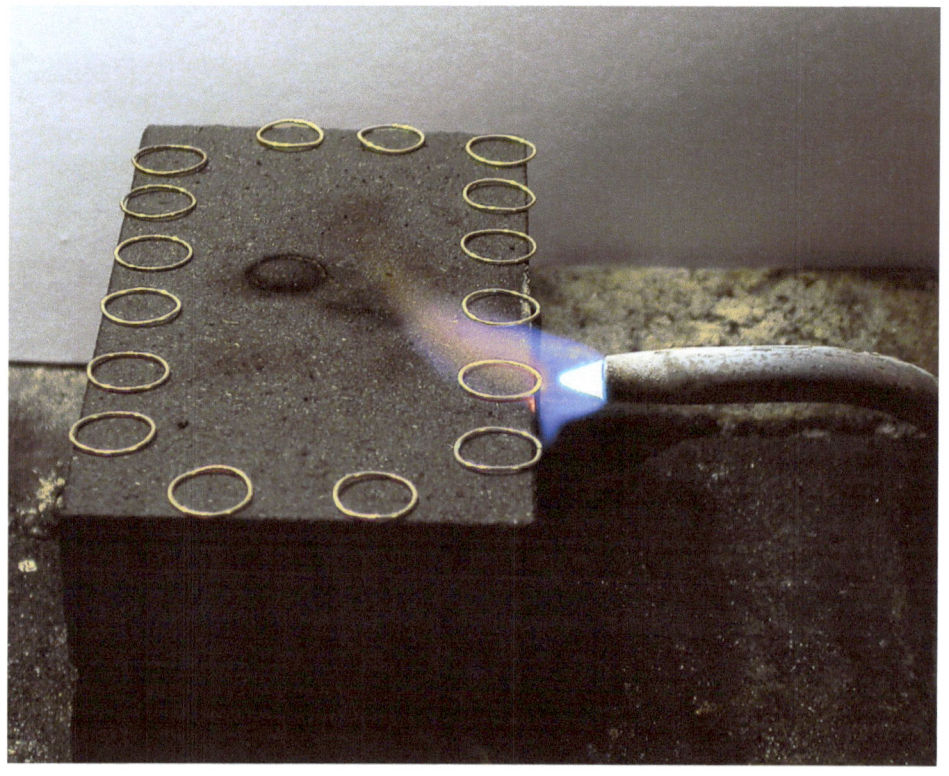

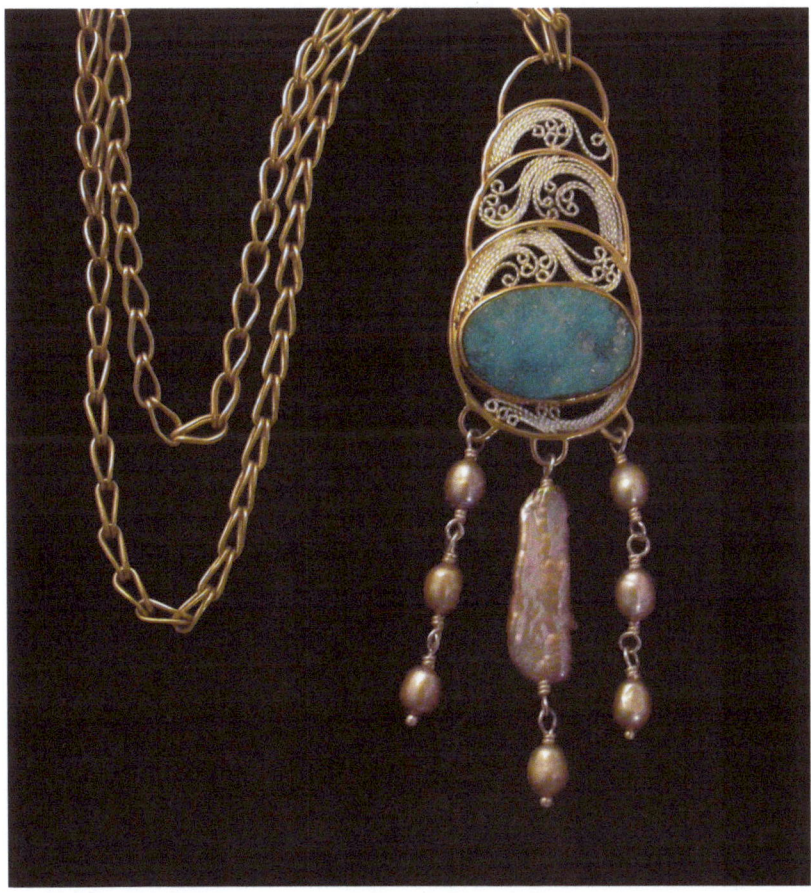

Moon Phases

Russian filigree and 1-Direction Single-Weave necklace; 18k, 22k gold, sterling silver, fine silver, chrysolcolla drusy; pendant: 2-1/2' long x 1" wide, 16" chain; 2006

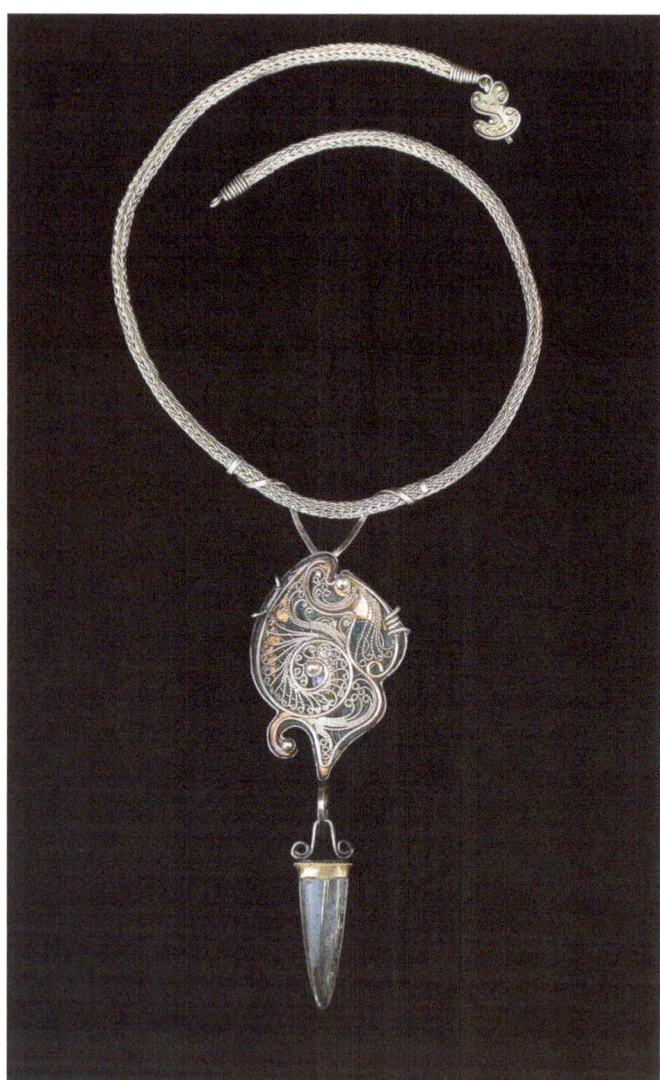

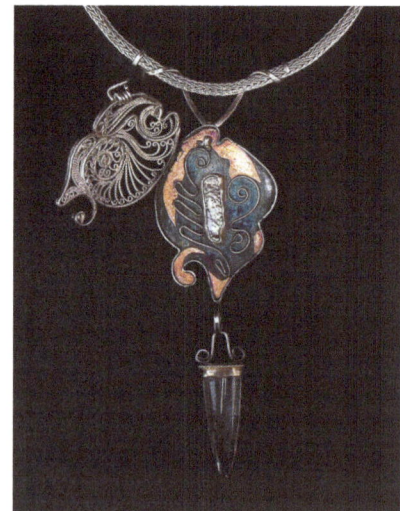

Pearls of Wisdom

Russian filigree, granulation, and kum boo amulet 2-Directional Double-Weave chain; 22k, 24k gold, fine silver, sterling silver, Baroque pearl, rutilated quartz; 3" long x 1-1/2" wide; 2000

Ancient Mediterranean Chain Patterns

1-Direction Single-Weave Loop in Loop

Metal & Mandrel:
22 gauge fine silver round wire, .25 oz for a 7" bracelet
10 or 11mm mandrel
1, 20 gauge solder filled sterling jump ring, soldered closed

There are many variations of this most basic loop in loop chain. To begin we will start with the symmetrical version that is beautiful by itself and also great with a pendant or used for a charm bracelet.

Other metal and mandrel possibilities:
24 gauge wire with 8.5 or 9.5mm mandrels
22 gauge wire with 9.5mm mandrel
20 gauge wire with 11, 12, or 13mm mandrels
14, 16, or 18 gauge wire with 19mm mandrel

Tip!

When experimenting with different wire gauges and mandrel diameters, make samples for future projects by weaving 3-4 links together and tagging them with the size information.

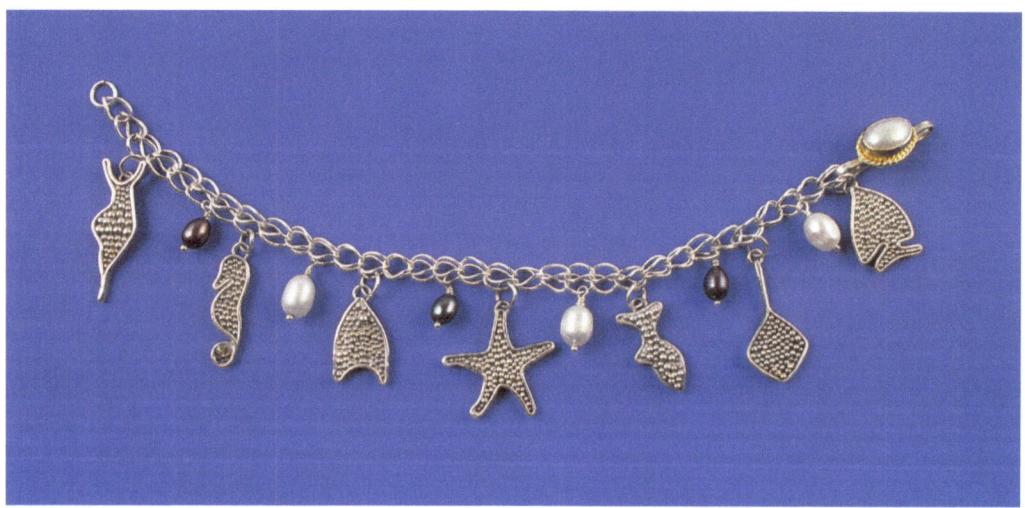

Underwater Landscape VI

Granulation and 1-Direction Single-Weave chain charm bracelet; 18k, 22k gold, sterling silver, fine silver, Biwa & freshwater pearls; 7" long x 1-1/4" wide; 1999; photo: Jennifer Clifton

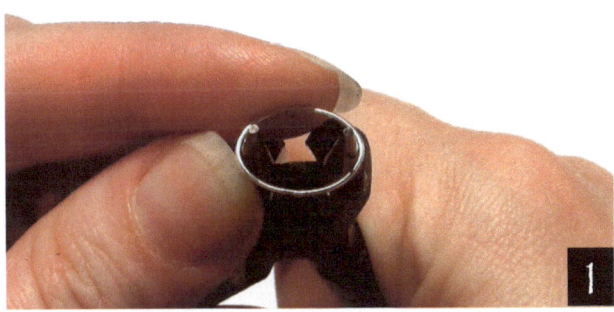

1 Place a link over round pliers and pull them open to elongate the link, making sure that the seam is in the middle, facing you (where it will receive the least stress).

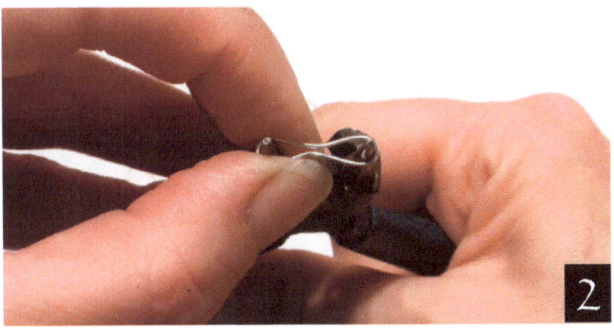

2 Pinch the link in the center to form an infinity symbol.

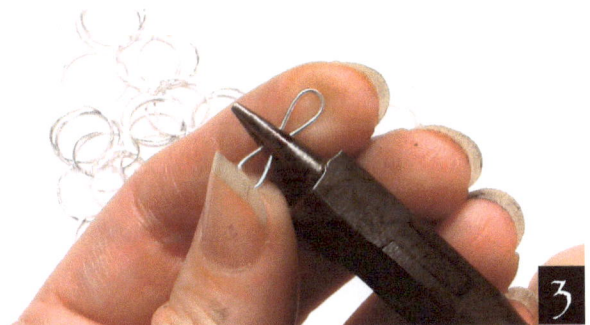

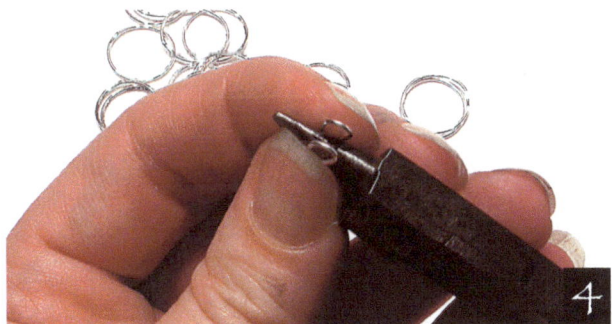

3-4 Gently hold the link with the pliers in the center and bend the loops into a 'U' shape.

Speed Things Up!

The key to creating an even chain is forming each link over the exact same spot on the pliers every time. Once you've established the place on your pliers that gives a rounded symmetrical shape to the link, mark the spot with a permanent marker.

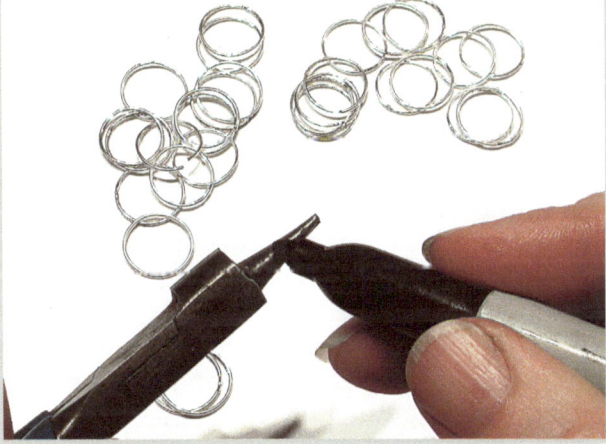

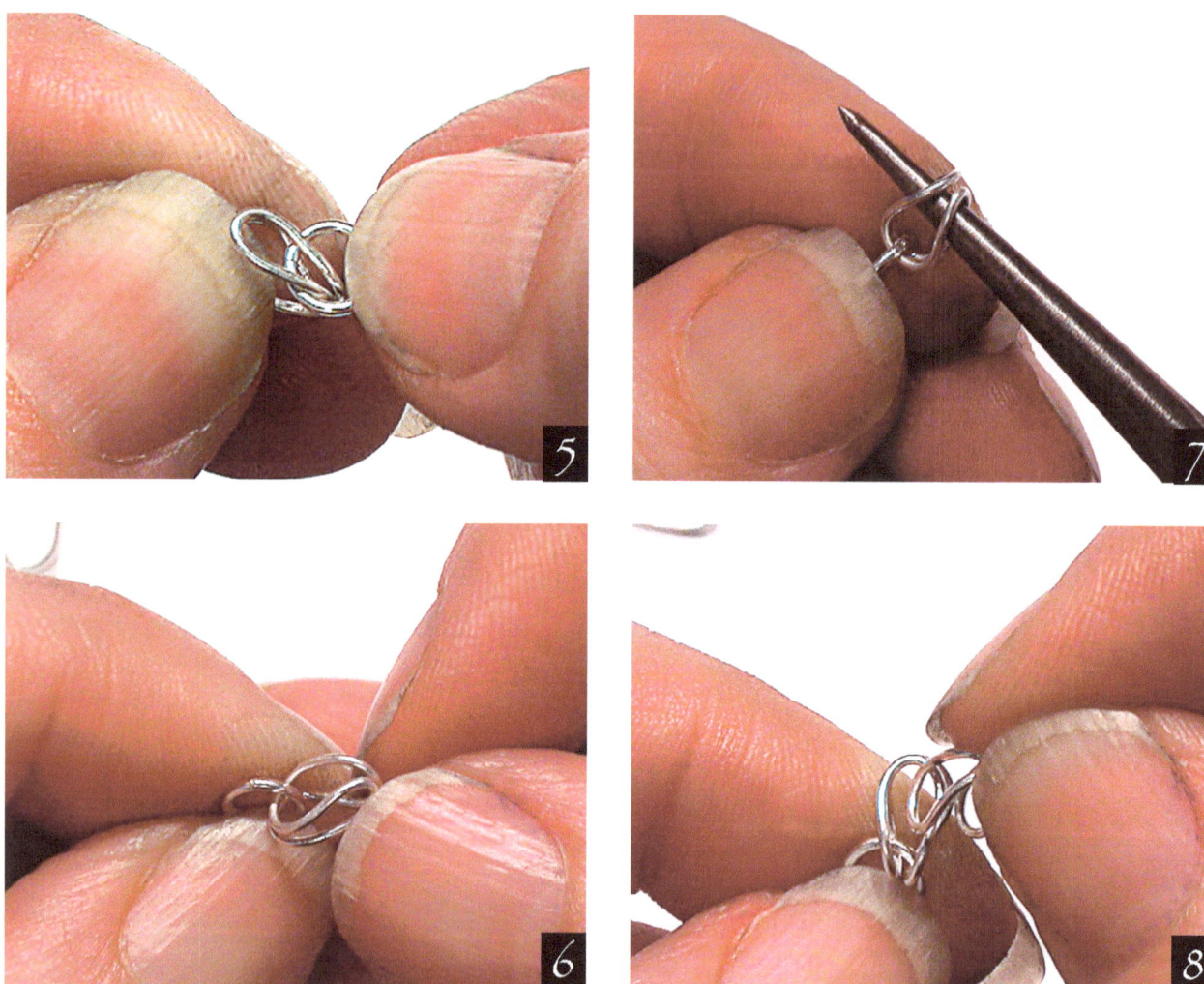

5-7 Thread a soldered closed jump ring onto one link. You may need to pinch one loop closed to push it through the jump ring. Pinch the tips of the loops together. If you pinched one loop to slide it through the jump ring, open it back up with a scriber. (Starting with a jump ring is easier than soldering one onto a finished chain.)

8 Thread another link through both loops that have been pinched together. Next thread a third link through the pinched loops of the second link. Note: Use only links that are well fused with no blobs or thin spots (page 15). If the chain breaks, you will have to take it apart and re-weave from the break.

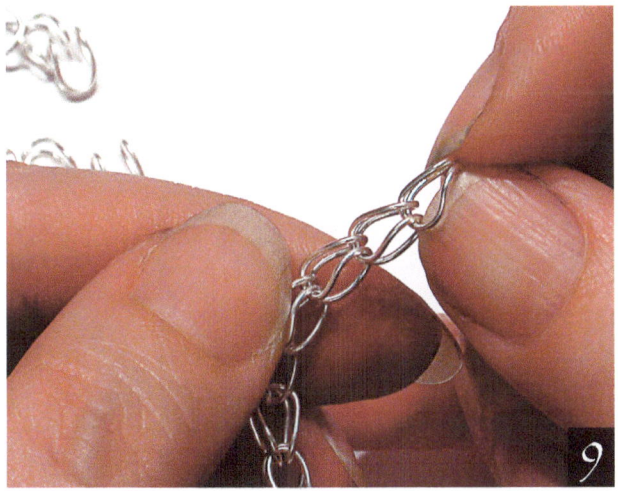

chain, insert the scriber the same depth into the next link, and twist it. Continue inserting and twisting the scriber at the same depth into each link all the way to the end of the chain. After the last link, turn the chain over and work your way back down the other side. Repeat the process on the other two sides of the chain as well. This trick will open all sides of each link the same amount and will make the links look uniform.

Basic Clasp

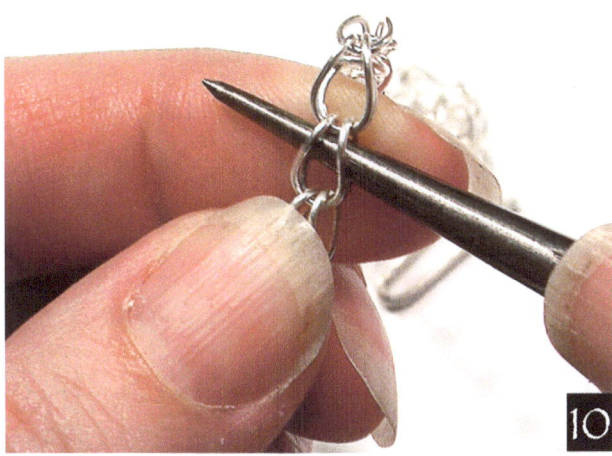

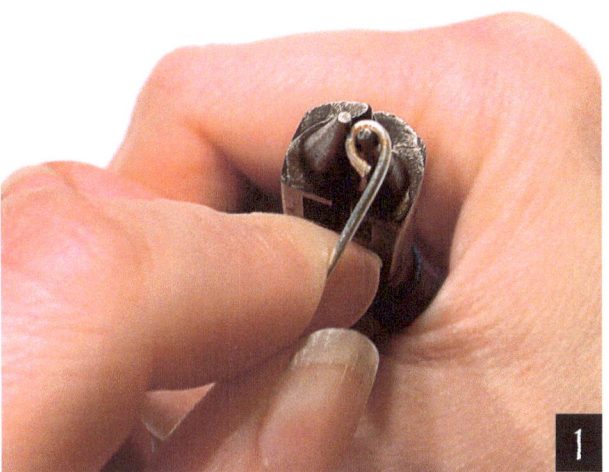

9 Continue weaving loops in loops until the chain is just long enough to wrap around your wrist. The clasp will create enough slack to put on the bracelet easily.

10 To make the chain even, insert a scriber into one side of the first link, and twist it. Continuing up this side of the

1 Always use sterling silver or 18k or lower gold for clasps and hooks. Fine silver is much too soft for clasps and jump rings. You can use 14 or 16 gauge round wire that has been slightly flattened in a rolling mill or 12 gauge half round wire as is with the rounded profile to the outside. Make a small loop at one end of the wire.

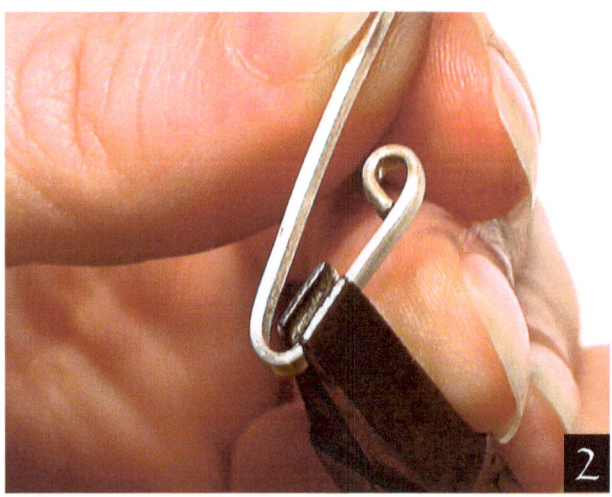

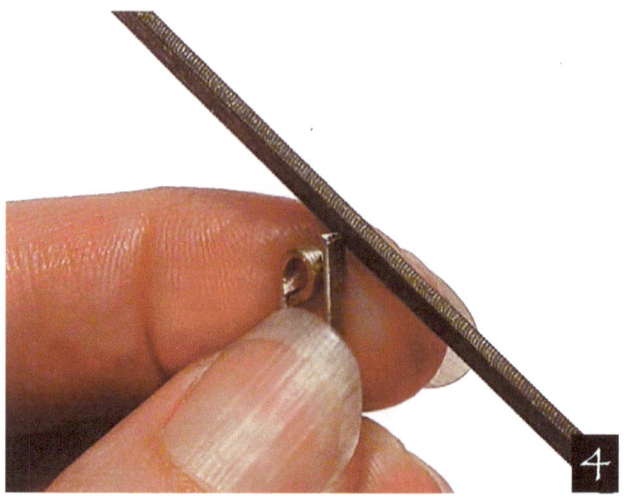

2   Hold the wire with flat pliers approximately 5/8" past the loop, and bend the wire around the pliers.

4 File the end of clasp so that the edges are not rough.

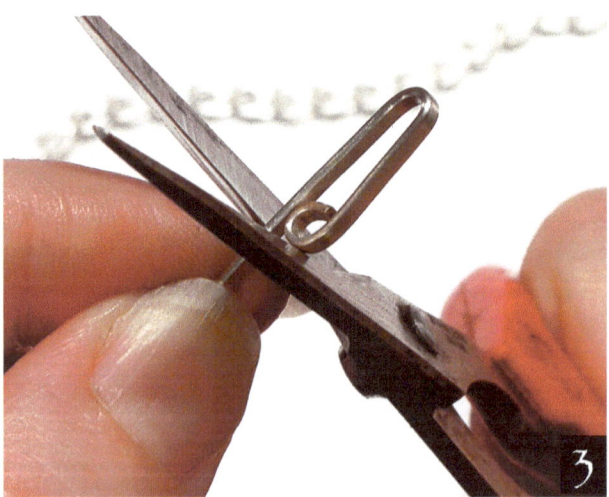

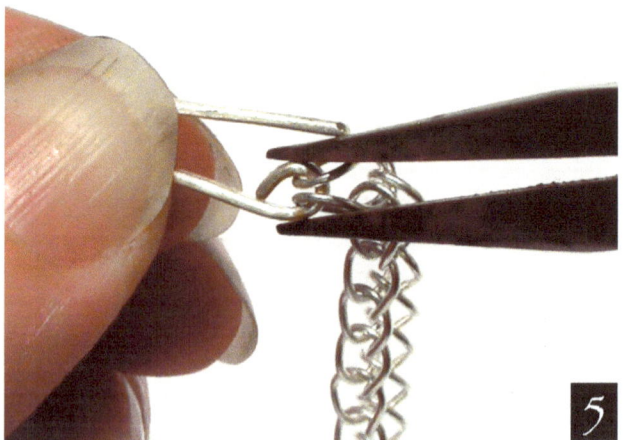

3 Cut the wire even with the end of the loop.

5 Open the loop with round pliers, and hook it through both loops on the last link of your chain. Close the loop with flat pliers.

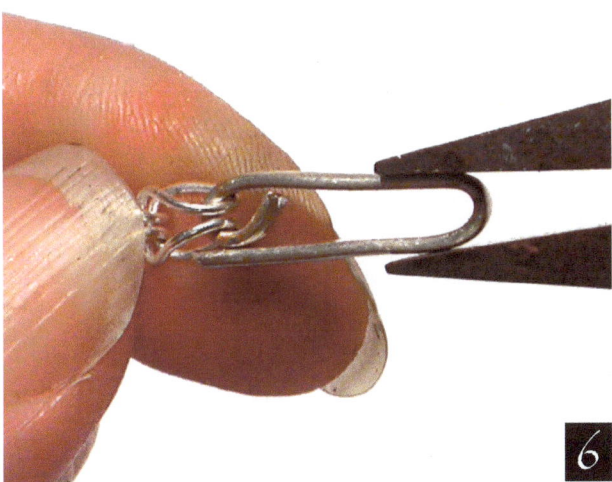

6   Gently squash the curve of the clasp with flat pliers so that the filed end of the wire is pressed against the loop with no space between them.

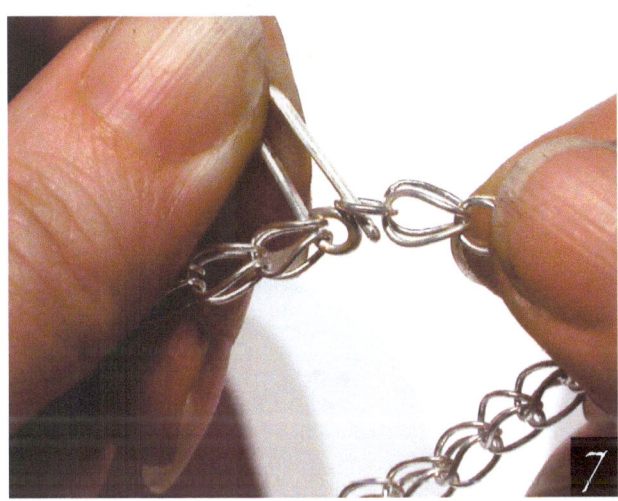

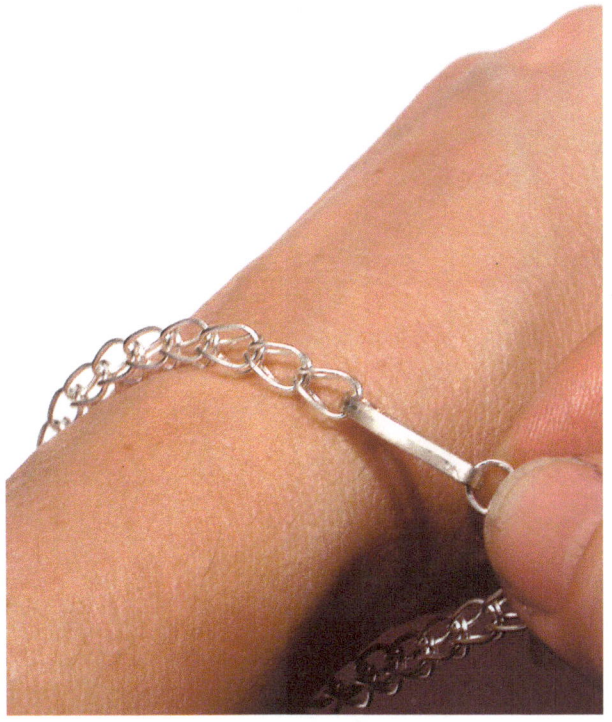

7   Now you have created a tension spot that will *click* when slid over the jump ring and will keep the jump ring from accidentally slipping through the clasp. For more decorative options, see the clasp in the Vertebrate chapter (page 54).

1-Direction Single-Weave Variations

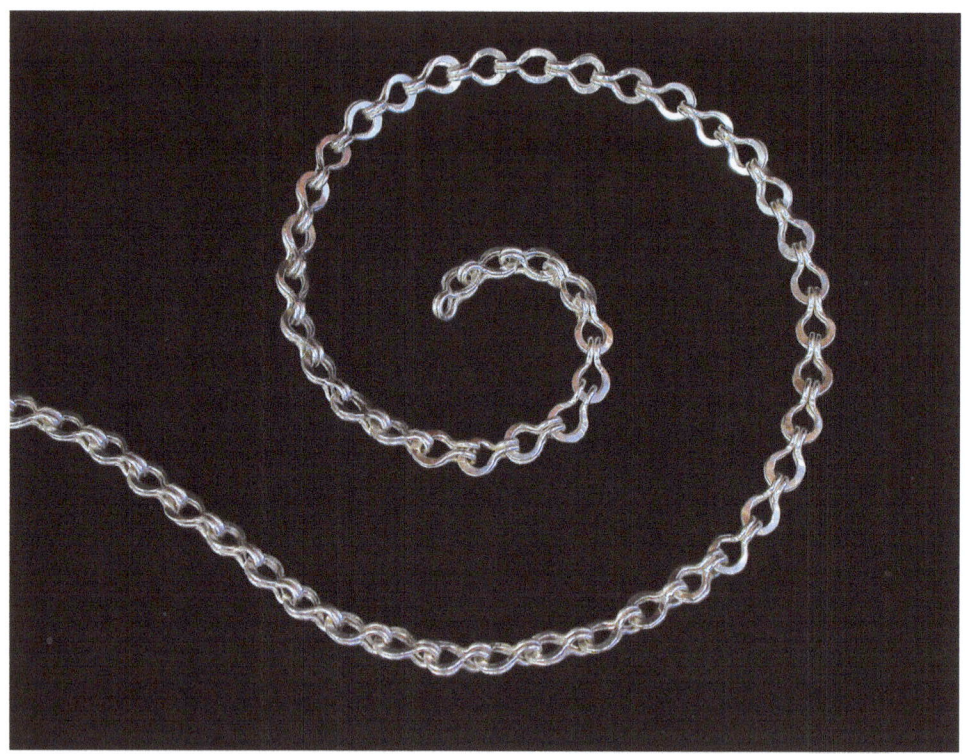

Pete Macko, Diane's Chain
Forged sailor's chain; fine silver, sterling silver; 16" long x 7/16" wide

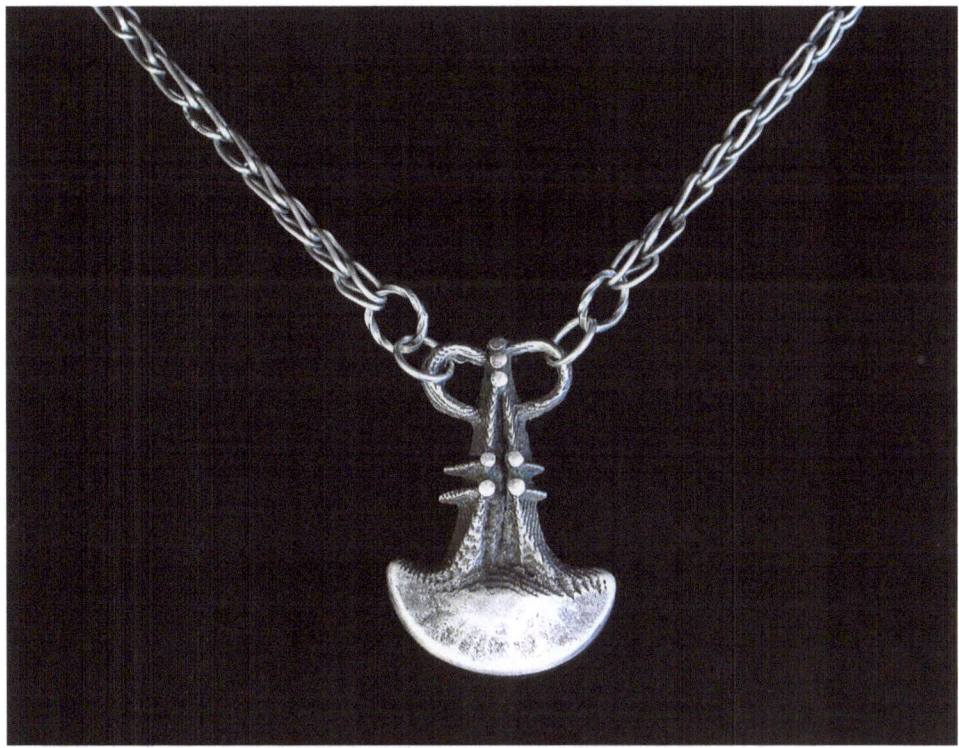

Corrina Sephora Mensoff, David's Hammer of Thor

Hot forged cuttlefish casting on an elongated 1-Direction Single-Weave chain; Fine silver, sterling silver; 2" long x 1-1/2" wide, 22" chain

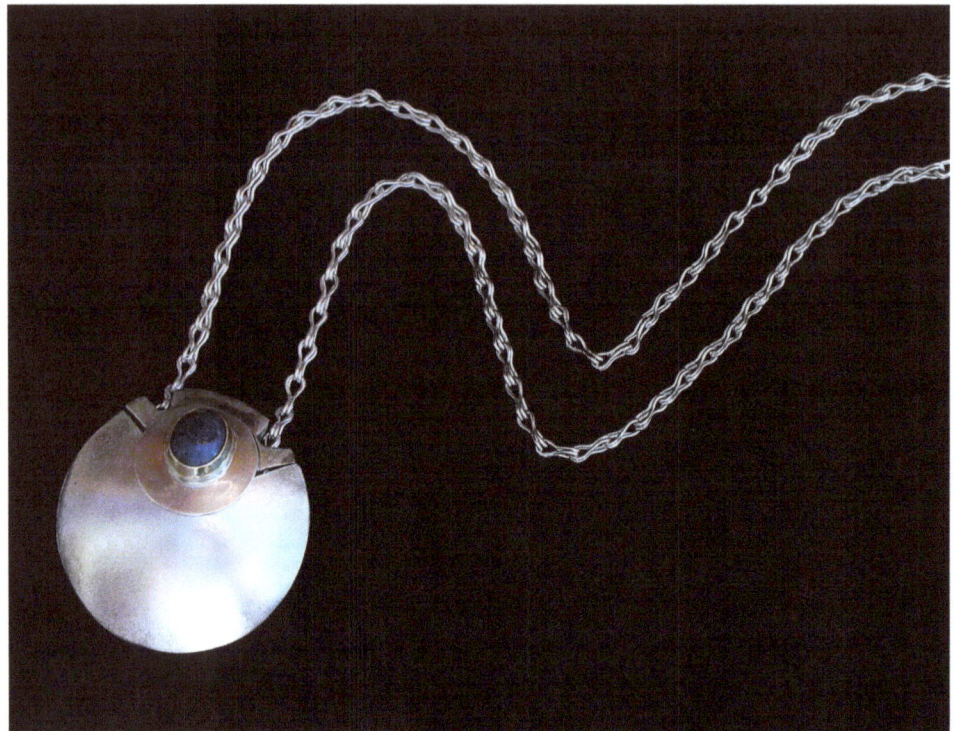

left: Pete Macko, Amulet

Hollow constructed amulet on a sailor's chain; Fine silver, sterling silver, lapis lazuli
1-3/4" diameter x 1/2" deep, chain: 26" long

bottom: Pete Macko, sailor's chain links; fine silver various sizes

A myriad of variations can be achieved by altering the size or shape of the links. For elongated chains place the link higher up on round pliers to form a longer and narrower infinity symbol shape. For a heavier chain such as Corrina Sephora Mensoff's necklace (page 23) consider thicker wire.

For variations such as Pete Macko's sailor's chains (above), after

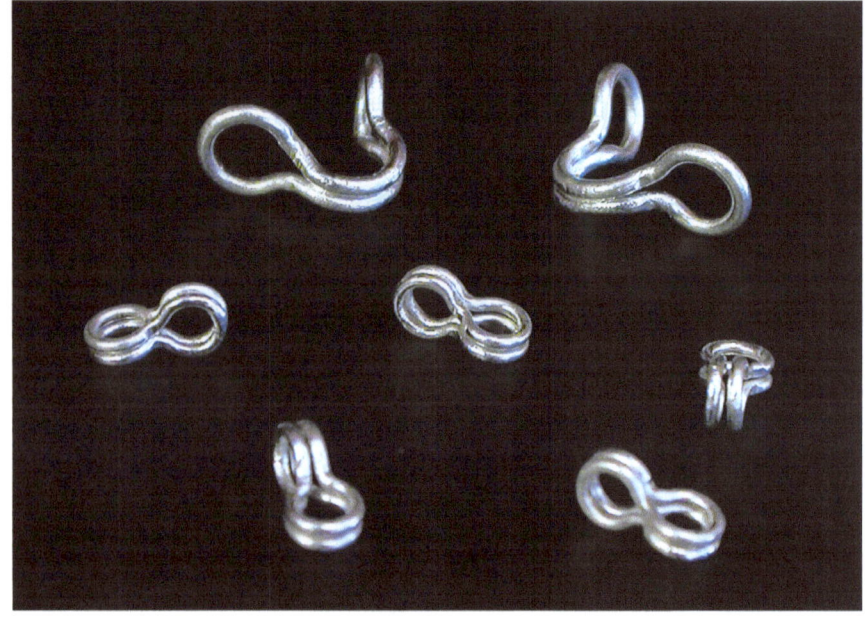

bending the link into a "U" shape, hold the loops at one end of a link with round pliers, and use a second pair of round pliers to pinch the link in the middle. Repeat the step, holding the link by the other end to make the pinched link symmetrical.

Larger links can also be pinched higher up and the loops forged, flared, and tapered with a planishing hammer such as in Pete Macko's *Diane's Chain* (page 24). The area that was the center of the infinity symbol shape should not be hammered, so that it does not become too thin.

For the striped effect in *Deep Blue* (right) alternate 22k gold and fine silver links in various patterns. See page 16 for how to fuse gold links.

Deep Blue is also an example of a chain that is connected directly to a pendant rather than run through a bail. Instead of starting with a jump ring, weave the first link into a loop on the pendant. You can weave from two separate loops drilled or soldered on the upper sides of a pendant or from a single one at the top. Two separate chains that are hooked by a clasp lay differently than one continuous

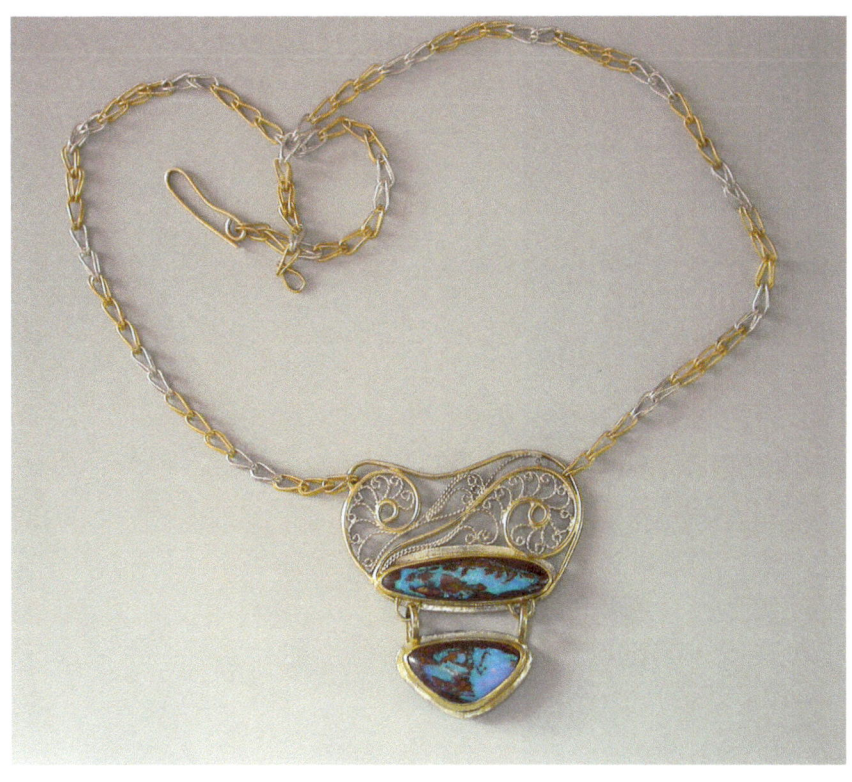

Deep Blue

Russian filigree pendant on a 1-Direction Single-Weave chain with alternating silver and gold links; 18k, 22k gold, fine silver, sterling silver, Koroit opals 1-3/4" diameter x 1/2" deep, chain: 26" long; 2005

chain. With two chains, you will not need a jump ring on the one without the clasp because it would make the chain twist when worn. Instead solder the last link closed with easy solder, keeping the torch away from the pendant.

One of the greatest advantages of using the 1-Direction Single-Weave pattern is that the basic clasp (page 21) will hook into any link, so that all necklaces and chokers can be adjustable.

Wrap Ties, Dangles, and Charms

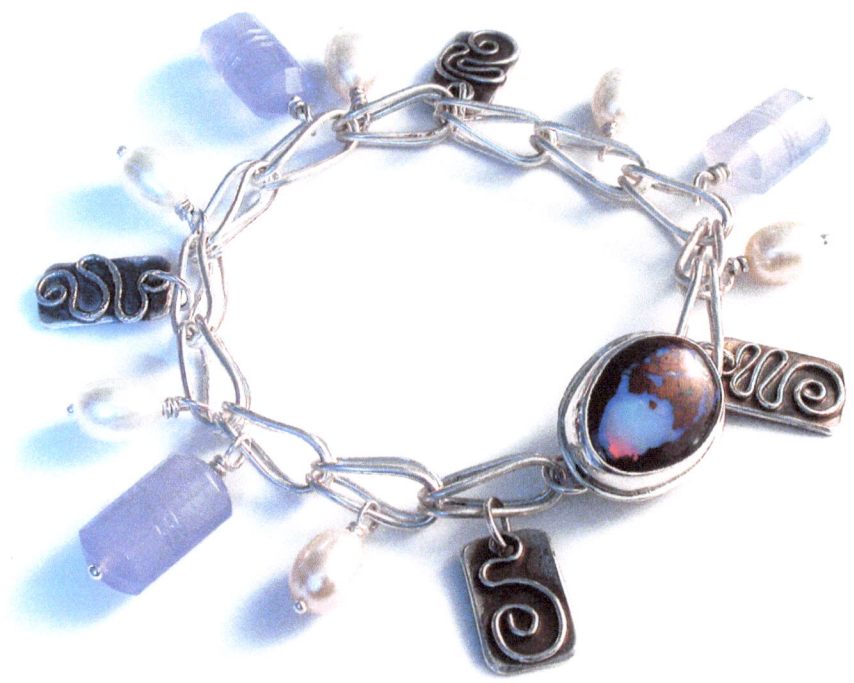

Strata Bracelet

A series of charm bracelets on 1-Direction Single-Weave chain, wire granulation charms;
22k gold, fine silver, sterling silver, Koroit opal, Biwa pearls, chalcedony; 2007

If made correctly, wrap ties can be very strong and durable. Always use the largest diameter wire that will fit through your bead to prevent it from breaking if the bead is accidentally caught on something. For long pendants or bracelets such as the Strata Bracelet (above), use 20 gauge fine silver round wire. (The links are 18 gauge wire with a 19mm mandrel.) For this bracelet, the pearls were re-drilled slowly with a regular drill bit to accommodate the thicker wire.

For chokers or shorter necklaces 22 gauge will work. For earrings, 24 or 26 gauge will work and will reduce the weight.

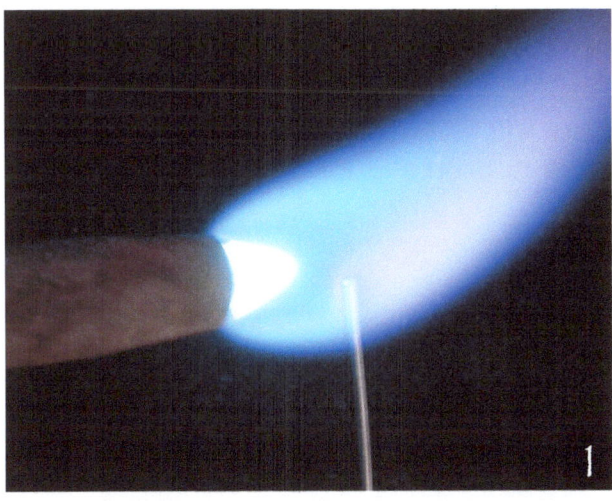

1 To make a head pin, cut a 2" length of 20 gauge fine silver round wire and hold it with tweezers straight up into the flame. The end will melt, forming a perfect ball.

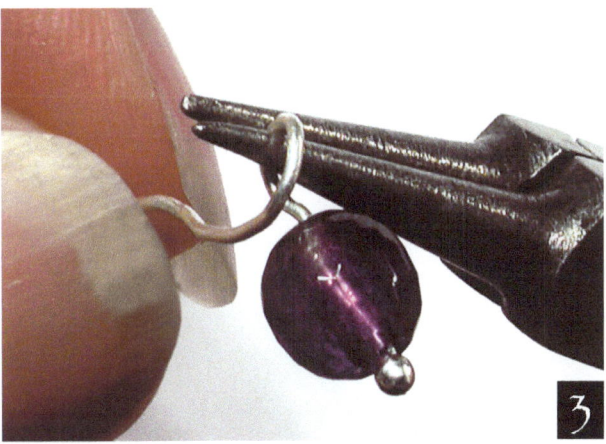

3 Wrap the wire back around the pliers to form a loop.

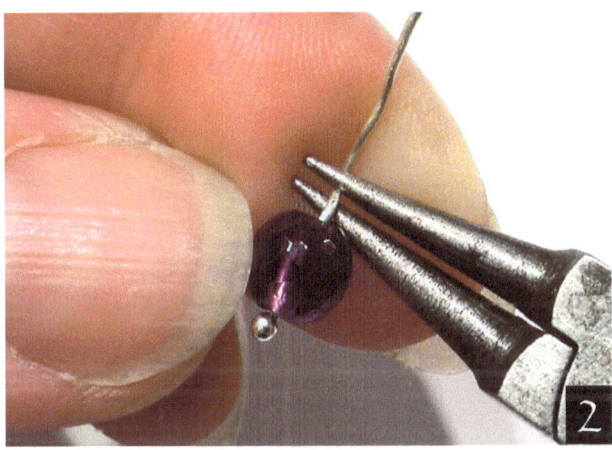

2 Thread a bead or pearl onto the head pin, and with round pliers, bend over the excess wire to almost 90 degrees.

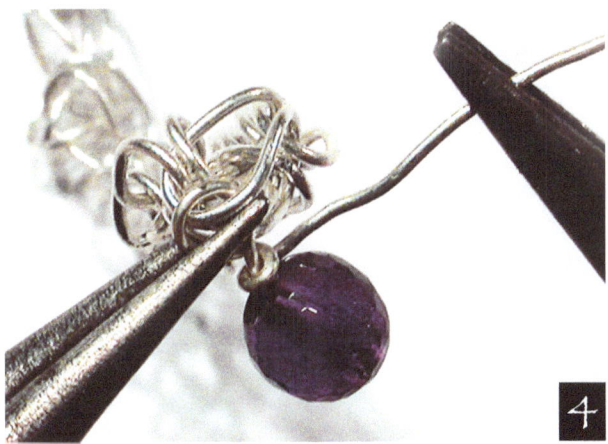

4 Attach the loop to a link, making sure that it lays along the same plane as the jump ring so that the dangles will hang correctly when worn. Note: How you want the dangle to hang will determine whether to attach the wrap tie to one or two sides of a link.

Holding the loop gently, wrap the wire two to three times between the loop and the bead. The wraps must lay tightly next to each other with no gaps between them.

When you have wrapped all the way down to the bead, making sure there is no space left, snip the excess wire with oblique or end cutters.

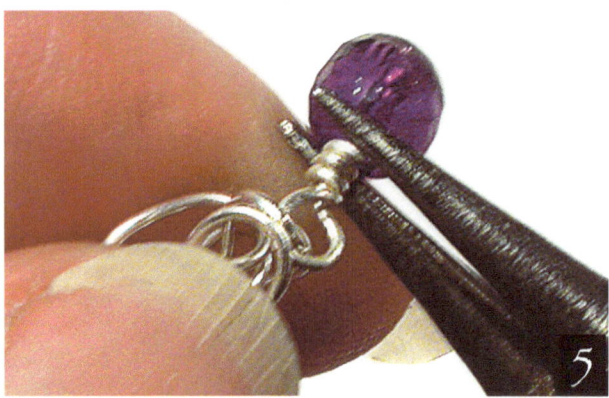

5 Very gently compress the end of the wire with the tips of round pliers so that it can't pull out or snag clothing. Be careful not to use much pressure, or you will deform the wrap.

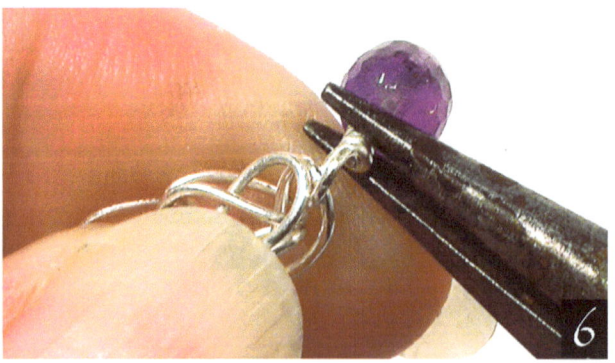

6 Also gently compress around the whole wrapped section with the tips of chain nose pliers to work harden the wire. Any gaps will be places that can bend and will eventually break.

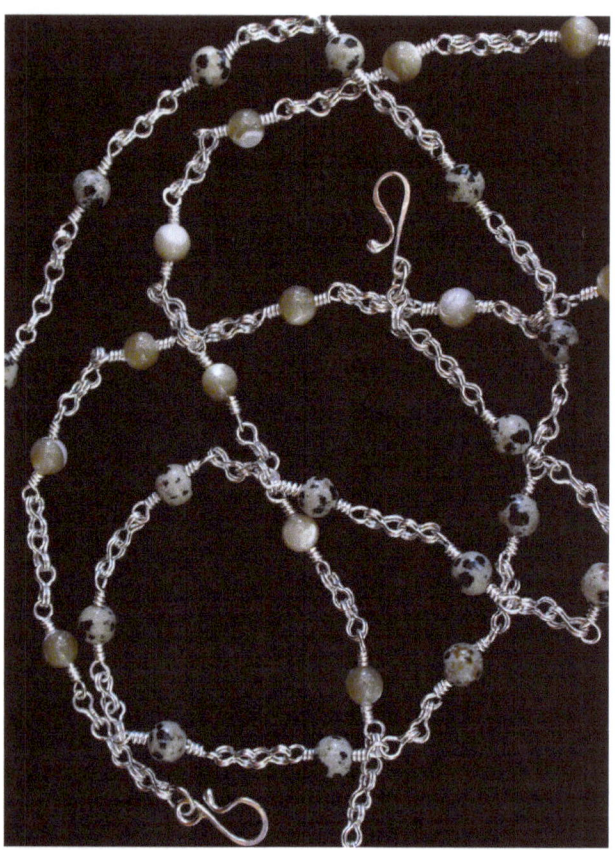

Pete Macko, various sailor chains with wrap tied beads
Fine silver, sterling silver, dalmatian jasper, agate

Another variation is, instead of making head pins, wrap tie both ends of the wire to join together links or other wrap tied beads.

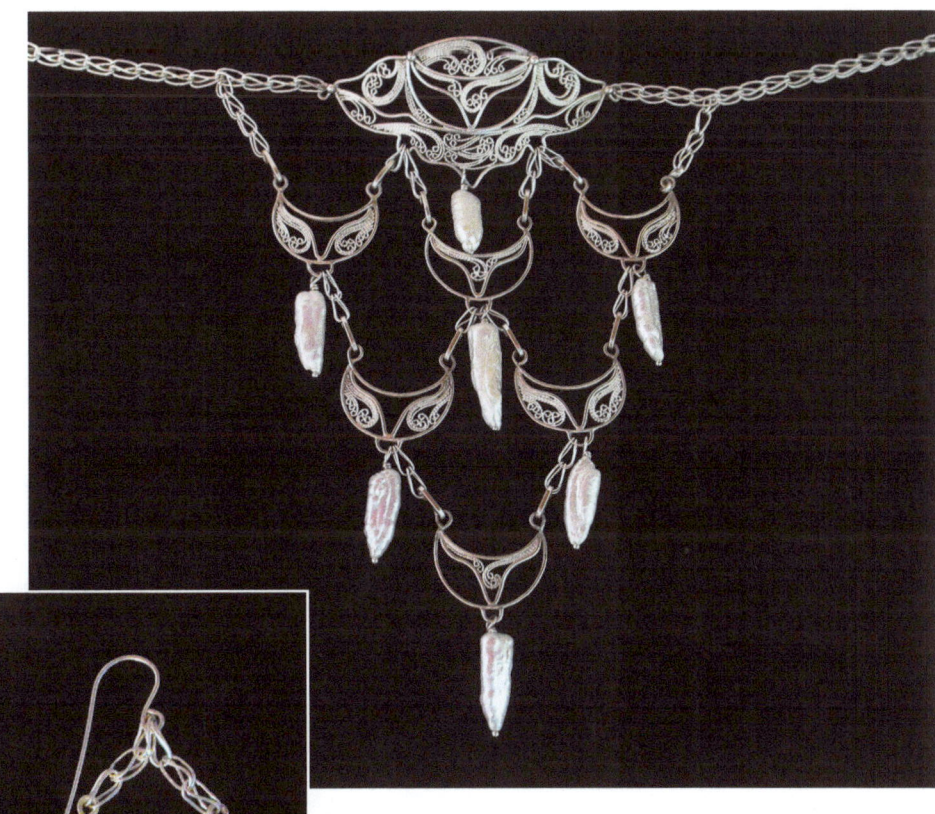

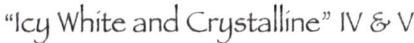

"Icy White and Crystalline" IV & V

Russian Filigree and 1-Direction Single-Weave chain
earrings and choker; fine silver, sterling silver, Baroque
and Biwa pearls
necklace: 6-3/4" from top center section of filigree to
bottom of longest drop, chain adjustable to 16"
earrings: 3-7/8" long 1" wide; 2006

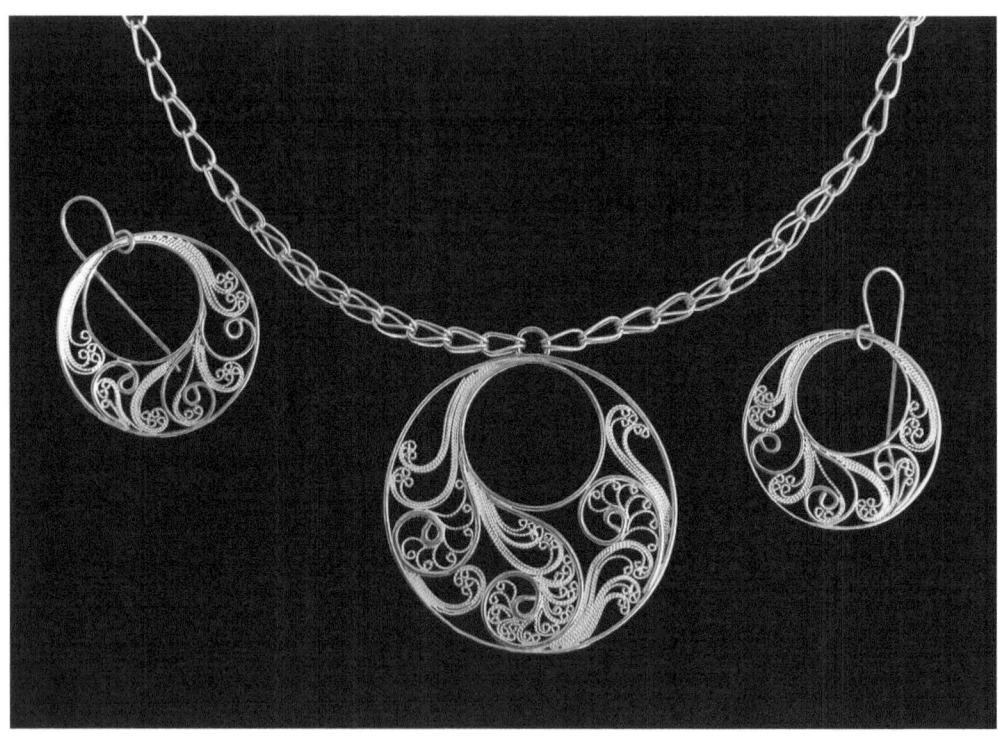

Deco III & IV

Russian Filigree earrings and pendant on a 1-Direction Single-Weave chain; fine silver, sterling
silver, earrings: 1-3/8" in diameter; pendant: 2" in diameter, chain adjustable to 16" long; 2007

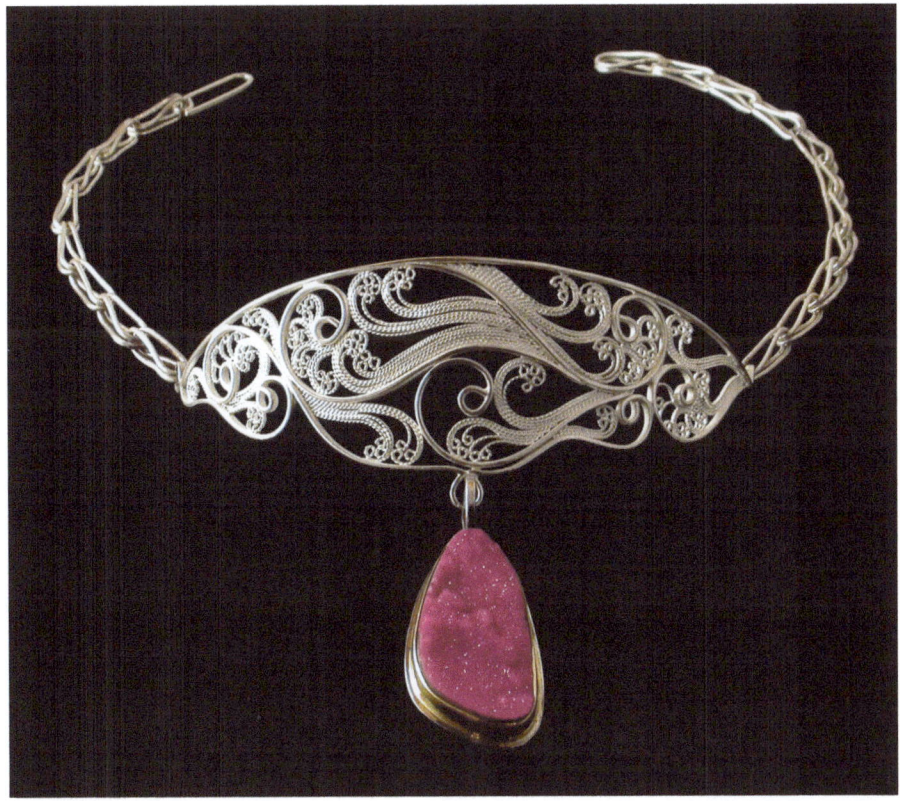

Undulation III

Russian Filigree and 1-Direction Single-Weave choker; 22k gold, fine silver, sterling silver, dolomite; adjustable to 16" long x 3" wide; 2006

1-Direction Double-Weave

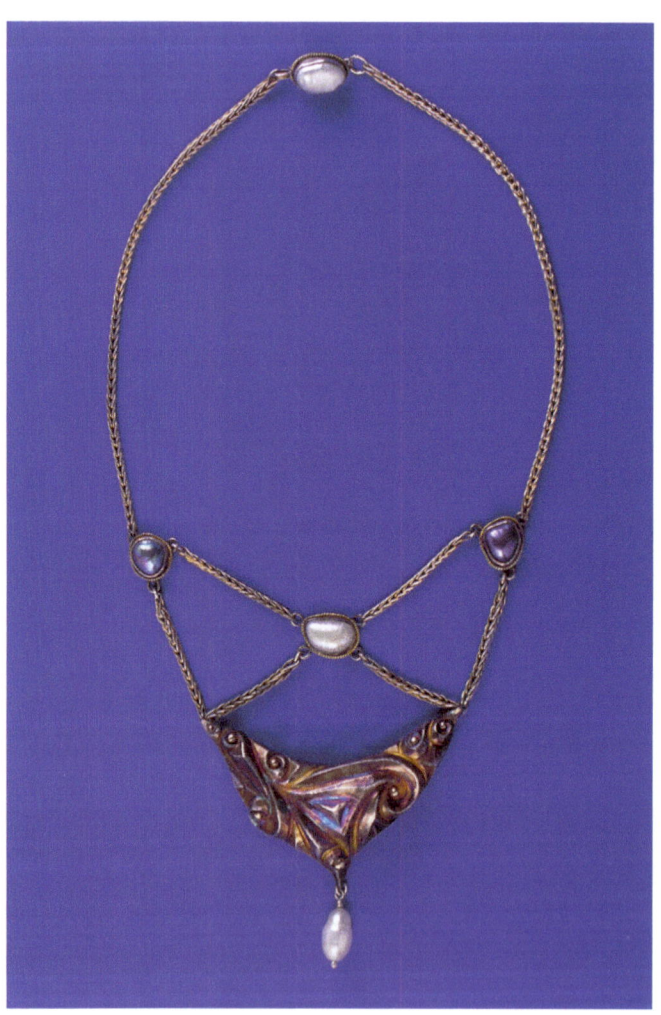

Metal & Mandrel
22 gauge fine silver round wire,
   .5 ounces for a 7" bracelet
10 or 11mm mandrel
1, 20 gauge solder filled sterling
   jump ring, soldered closed

This chain weaves into a fine braided square. Because it is woven only from one direction, it does not require end caps or other special endings, which makes it easy to hook to itself or to other components.

"Amidst the Lantern Light"

High relief Eastern repoussé and 1-Direction Double-Weave chain necklace; Sterling silver, fine silver, 18k gold accents, Biwa & freshwater pearls; 9-1/2" long x 3-7/8" wide; 1998 photo: Jennifer Clifton

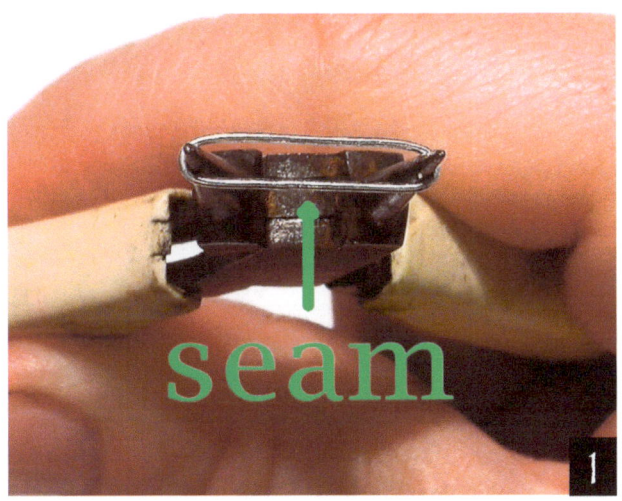

1 Place a link over round pliers and pull them open to elongate the link.

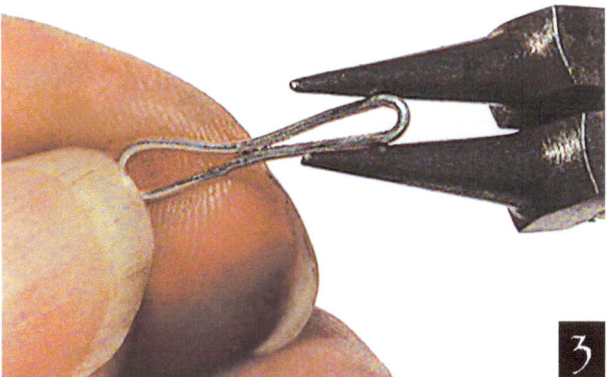

not bend the link into a "U" shape before weaving.)

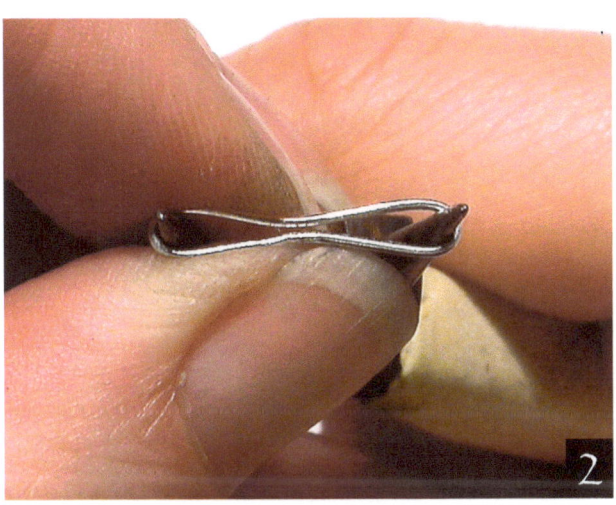

2 Pinch the link in the center to form an infinity symbol shape.

3 Gently Pinch one end of the link so that it will be easy to insert when weaving. (Do

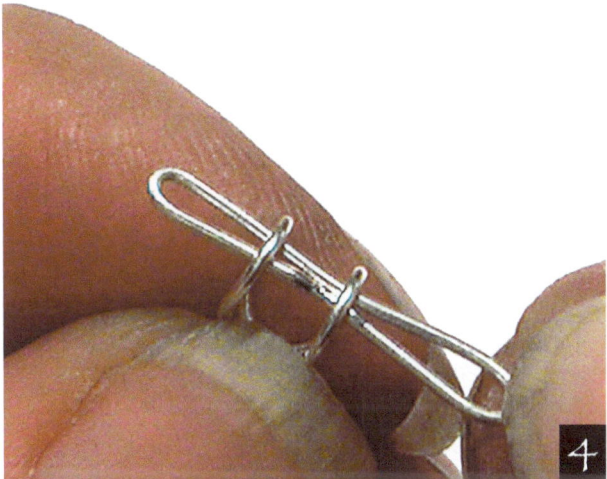

4 Thread a soldered closed jump ring onto one link, and bend the link into a "U." Thread a second link through the first, bend it into a "U" and pinch it closed.

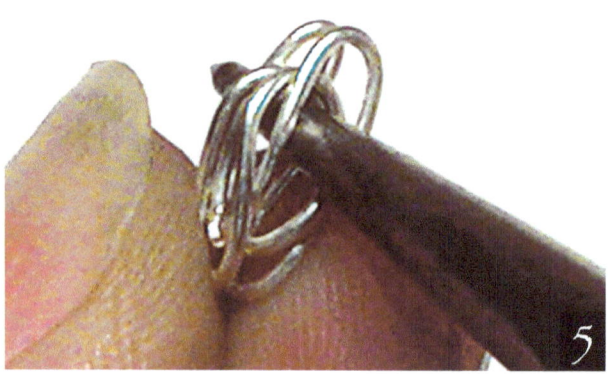

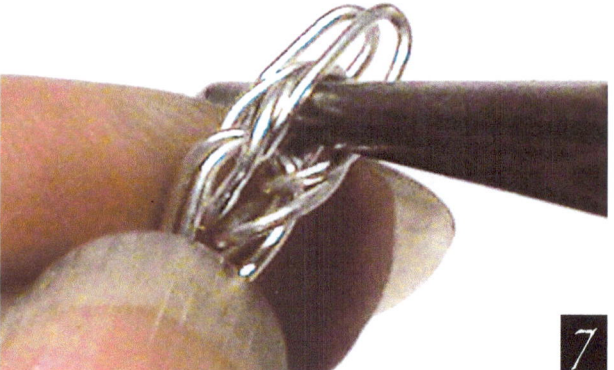

5 Scrunch the links so that the top one sits down inside the first one. Use a scriber to open a space in these two links.

7 Use the scriber to open up a space in the loops of the top two links.

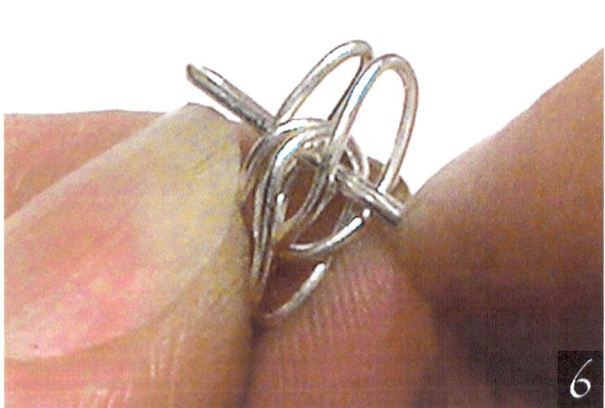

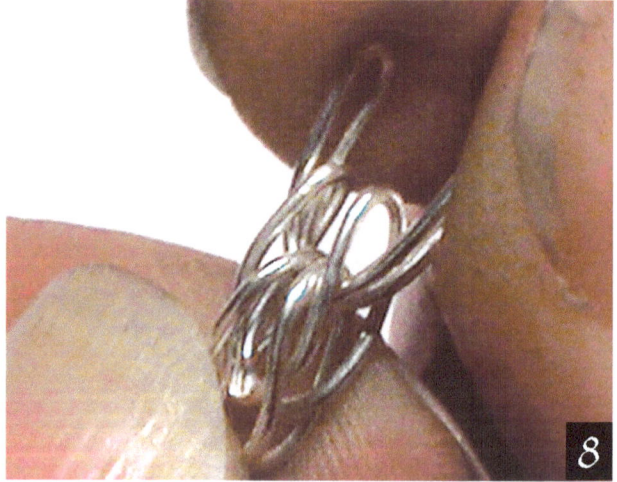

6 Thread a third link through both of the first two links, bend it into a "U" and pinch closed.

8 Weave a forth link through this space in the top two links. Weaving through one link at a time makes a chain a single-weave, which is more open. Weaving

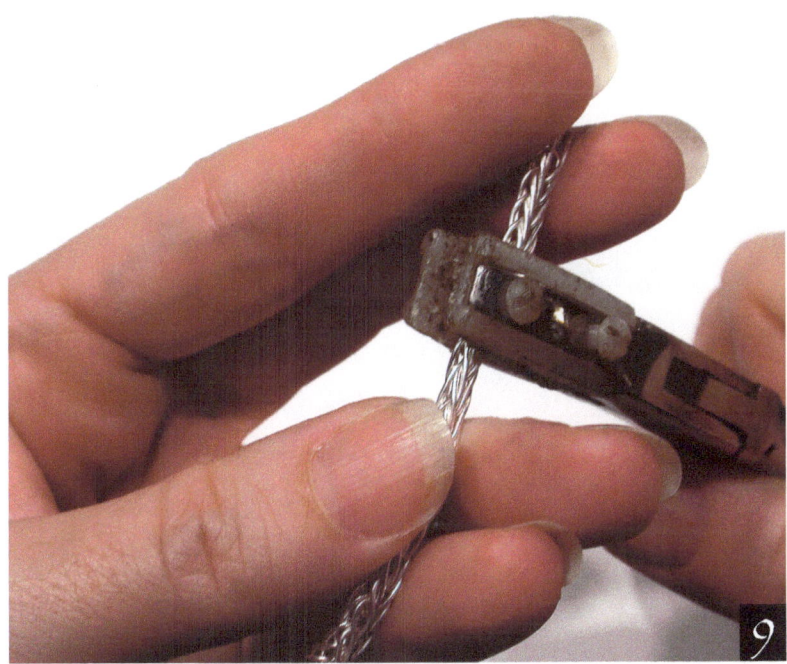

gently tapping along the length of all four sides with a rawhide mallet. This is the traditional way of evening the chain, but starting with the pliers gives more control.

The chain will increase slightly in length during this process so you can compress or hammer it as soon as you have woven four to five inches. To add on, use the scriber to open up the top two links, and continue weaving. Take care that you do not over compress the chain. There is no way to decompress it! Attach a basic clasp (page 23) to the final link.

through two links at a time makes it a double-weave, which makes it appear braided.

8 Continue weaving until the chain is almost the desired length.

9 Gently compress it with flat nylon pliers, working your way down all four sides of the chain.

10 Continue the evening process by

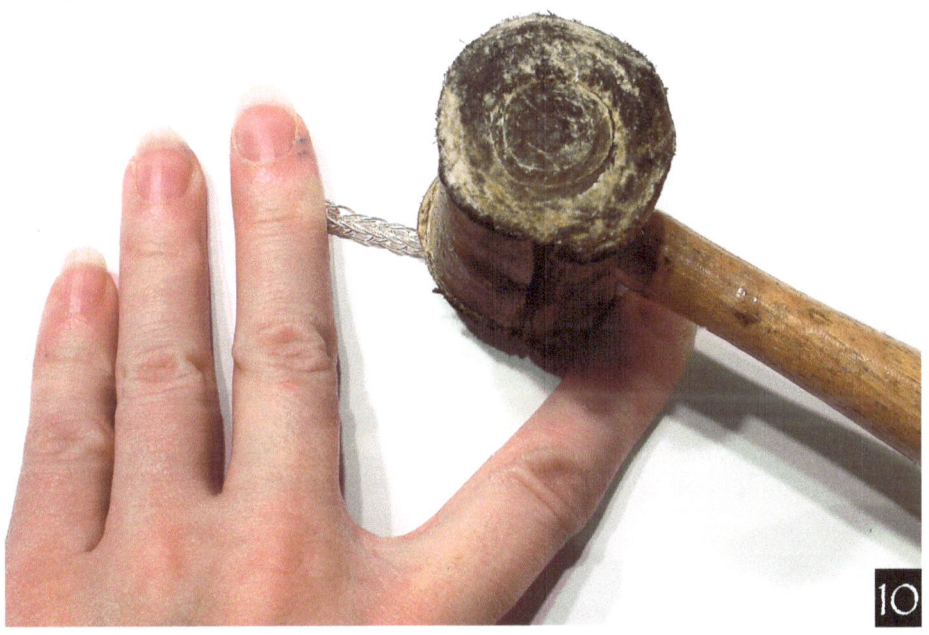

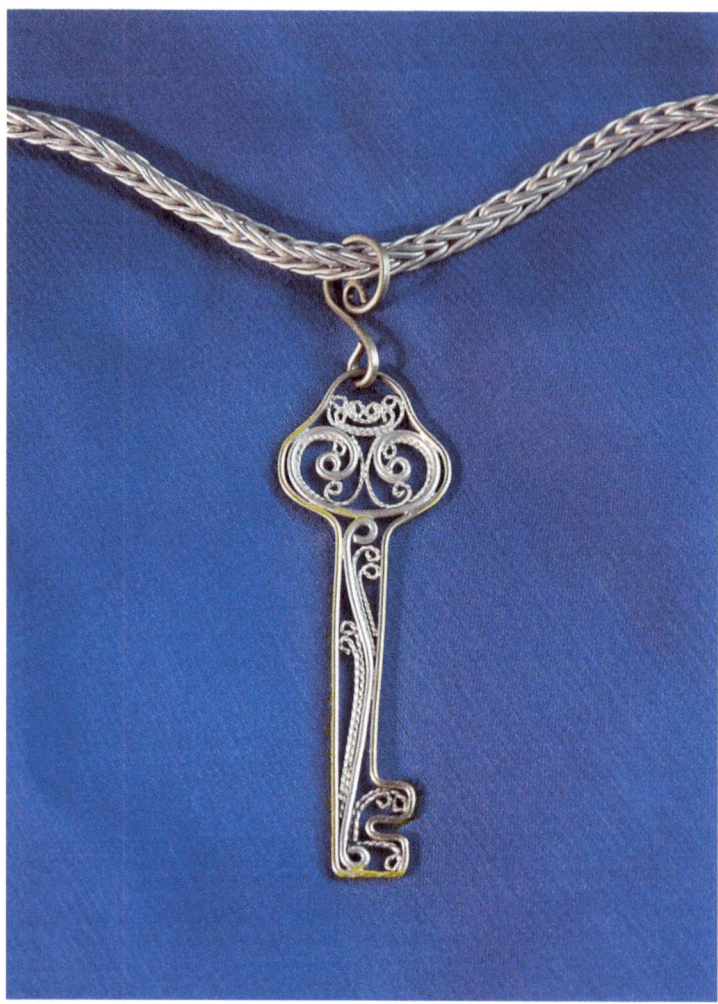

The Key

Russian filigree and 1-Direction Double-Weave chain necklace; 18k
gold, sterling silver, fine silver; 2" long x 5/8" wide; 2000

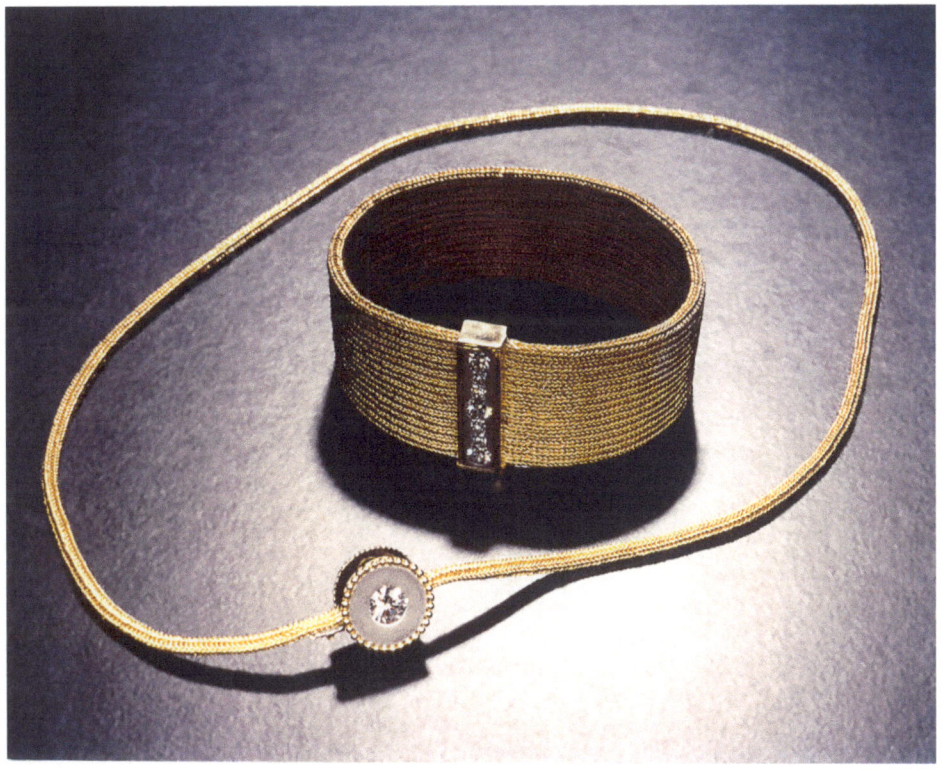

Kathy Kinev, Untitled
Granulation pendant on a 2-Directional Double-Weave chain, mesh chain bracelet; 18k,
22k gold, platinum, diamonds;
necklace: 5/8" diameter, 1/4" deep, 20", 3/16" wide chain
bracelet: 7-3/4" long x 1-1/4" wide; photo by the artist

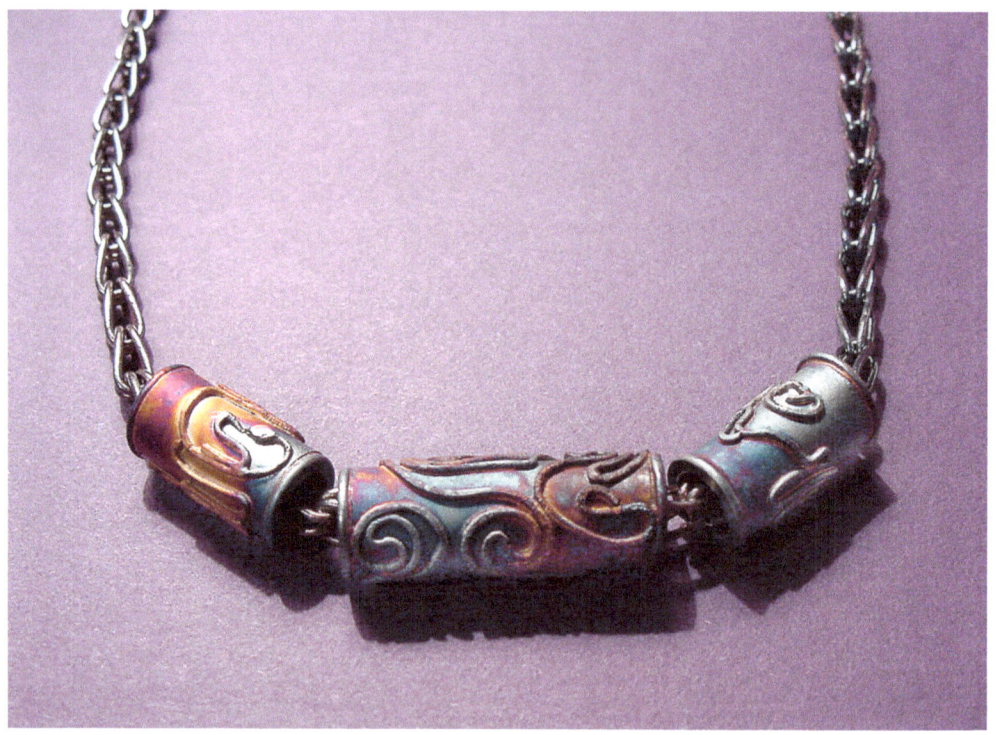

Peter's Beads

Wire granulation beads on a 1-Direction Single-Weave chain; fine silver, sterling silver, beads: 1-1/8" and 5/8" long x 1/2" in diameter, chain 22" long; 2003

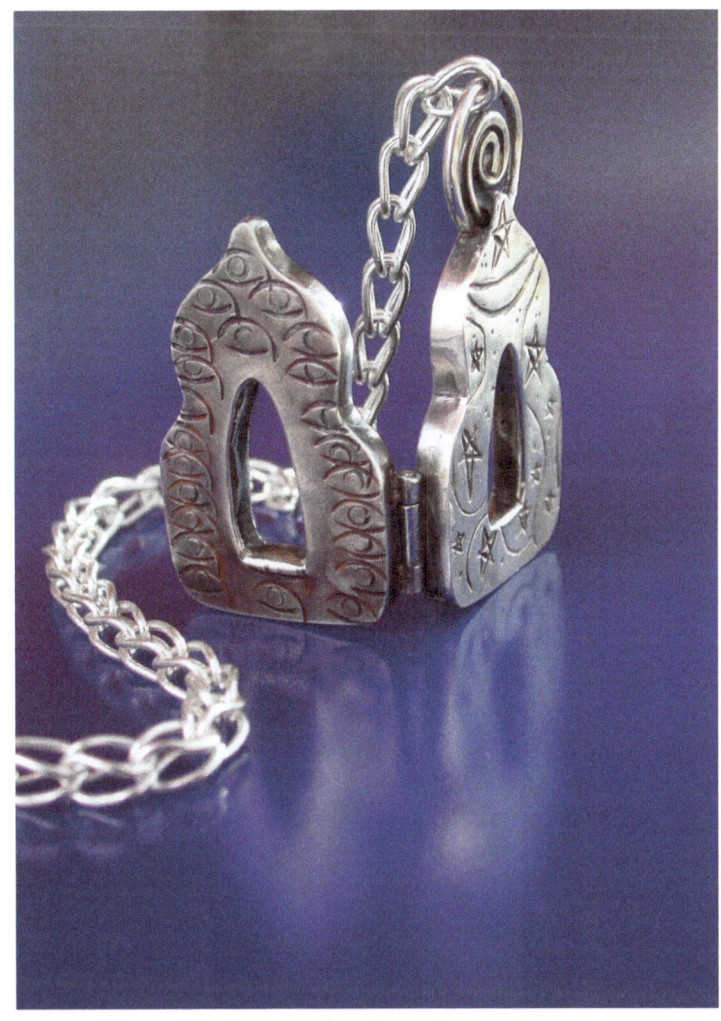

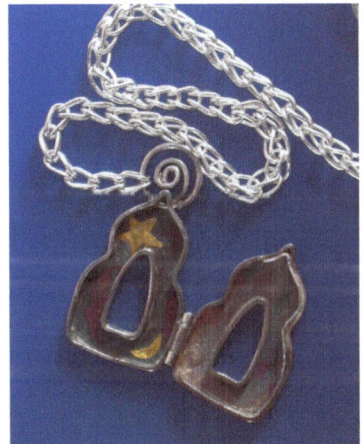

Temple of Love

Chased, kum boo, and fabricated amulet on a 1-Direction Single-Weave chain; fine silver, sterling silver, 24k gold; 1-3?4" long x 3/4" wide x 3/8" deep, chain 20" long; 2003

2-Directional Double-Weave

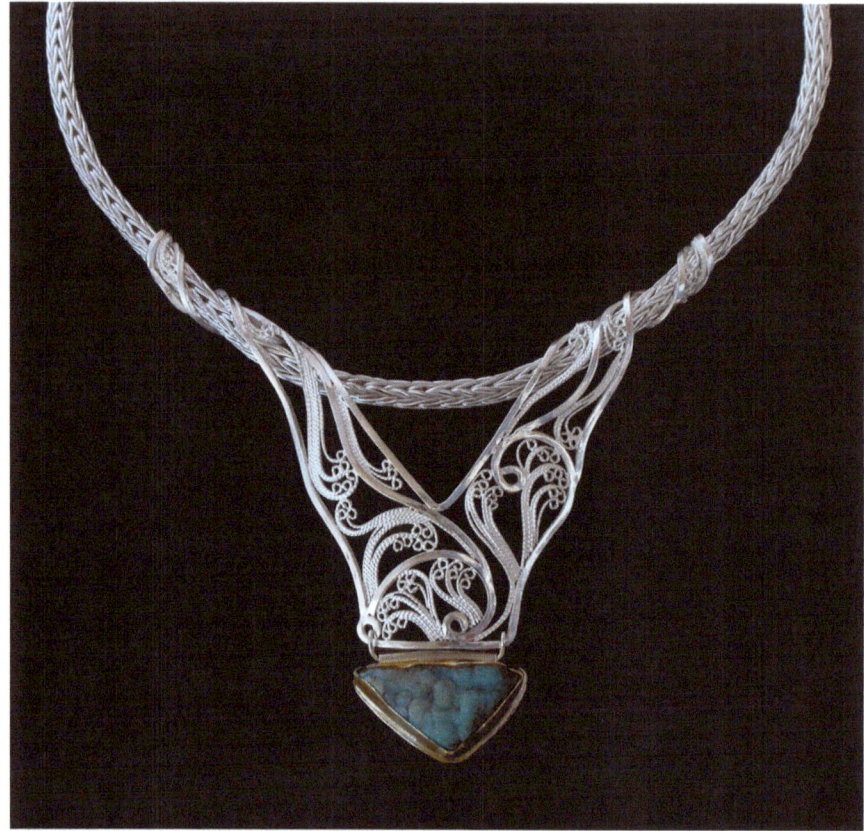

Entwine

Russian filigree
and 2-
Directional
Double-Weave
chain necklace,
sterling silver,
fine silver, 22k,
gold,
chrysocolla
drusy
pendant:
2-3/4" long x
2-3/4" wide,
16" chain
2007

Metal & Mandrel
22 gauge fine silver round wire,
    1 oz for a 7" bracelet
10mm or11mm mandrel

This chain appears to weave as a square
then gets hammered round. What creates
its herringbone pattern is that the links
are woven two at time like the 1-Direction
Double-Weave, and what makes it round is
that it is woven from two directions,
perpendicular to each other. Because
there are multiple loops at the end, they
must be covered by wrapping or end caps.

Forming the links
Set aside two links. For all the rest follow
steps 1-3 of the 1-Direction Double-Weave
pattern on page 36.

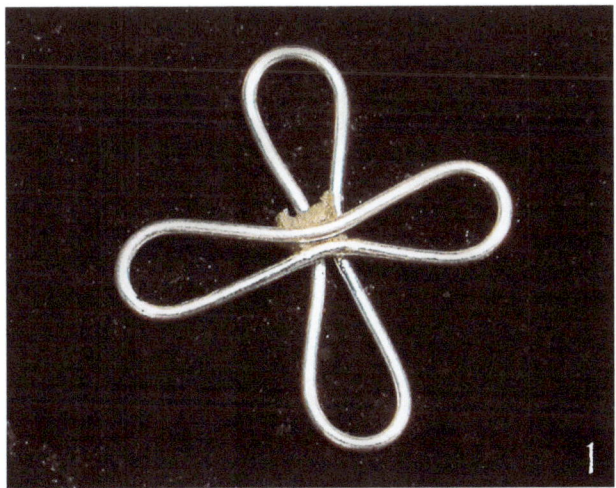

1 Form the two links that were set aside so they are open and symmetrical, and solder them with easy solder into a plus shape (paste solder shown but sheet or wire solder will work).

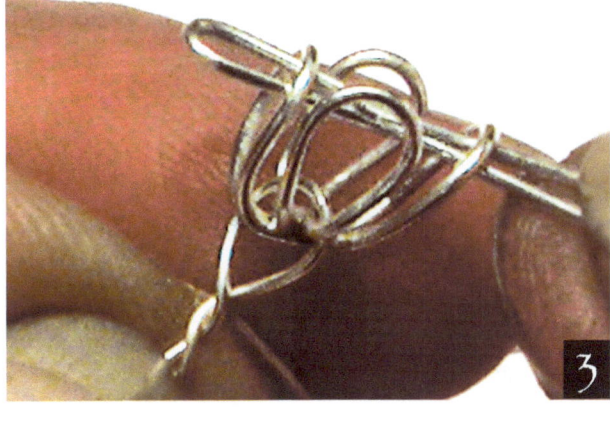

2 Bend the loops of the plus shape straight up. This set of starter links can be

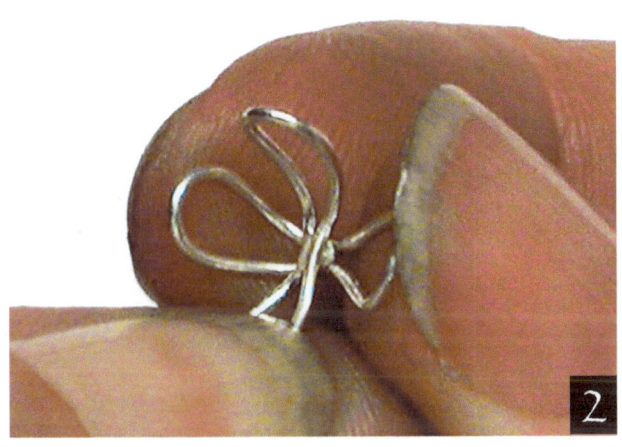

difficult to hold, so make a handle by twisting a piece of wire around the bottom.

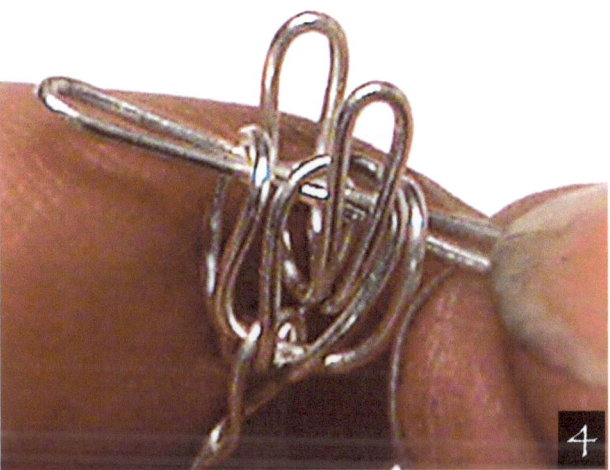

3-4 Weave a link straight across the loops that sit lower, and bend it into a "U" shape. Don't pinch it closed. Weave another link through the loops of the perpendicular direction.

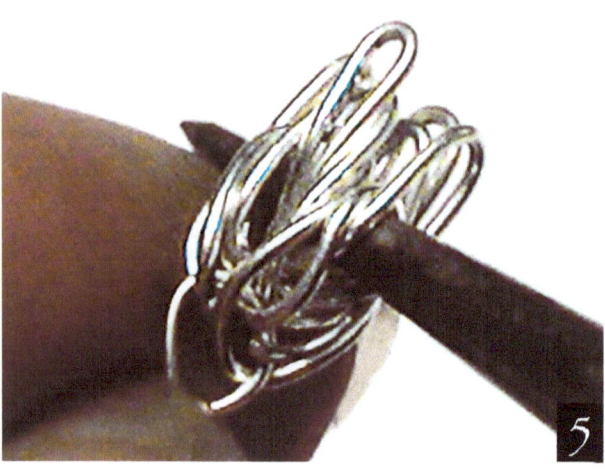

5 To open up a space to weave a link, insert the scriber straight through the top two sets of loops (two links) going the first direction you wove. Insert the scriber through the same links from the other side so that the loops are all opened evenly.

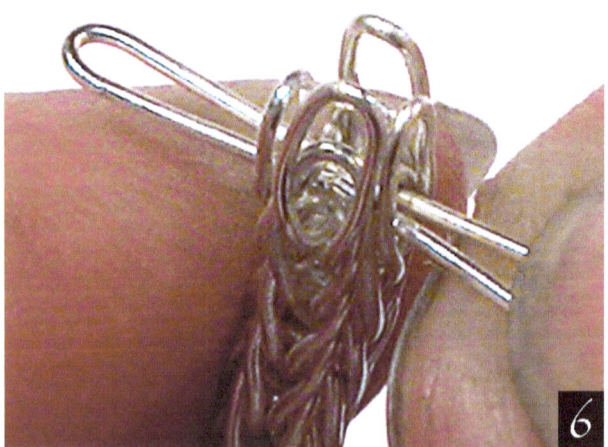

Weave a link through this opening. Repeat this step to weave a link through the

perpendicular direction.

6 Continue weaving links through the top two sets of loops from each direction.

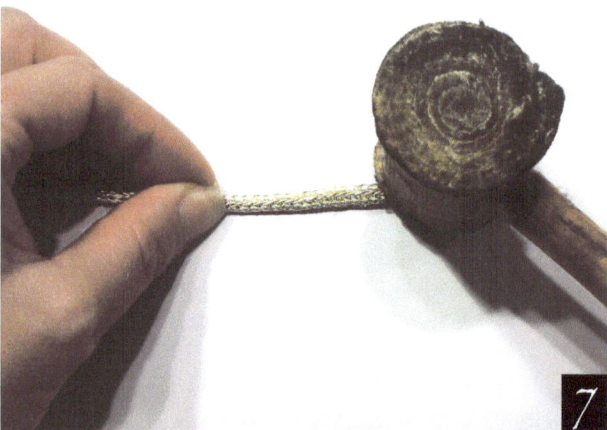

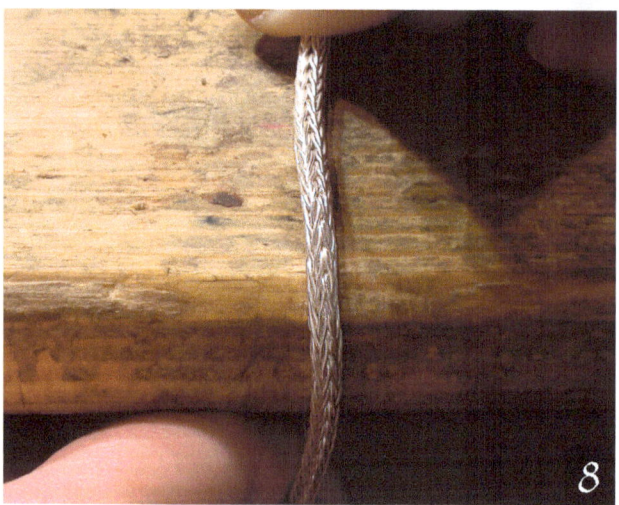

Always weave the next link from the direction in which the loops sit lower.

7-8 At any point when you have enough chain to hold, hammer gently with a rawhide mallet along the corners of the square to compress it, alternating corners frequently to keep the chain from becoming too squashed on one side. Once the chain becomes round, continue hammering up and down the length of the chain while rotating it to even out the diameter. Compressing the chain will stretch it, making it slightly longer.

8   Hammering may make the chain stiff. While rotating it, pull it back and forth along a beveled edge, such as the rounded edge of your workbench, to make it supple.

As a rule, these ancient style chains should not be pulled through a drawplate, however, if a chain needs to be just slightly smaller in diameter, and hammering isn't compressing it enough, it can be pulled through a wooden drawplate (or appropriate size hole drilled into a piece of wood). Be careful! To much drawing can misshape a chain, and there is no way to reverse the damage. The chains can be left as they are, polished with a mini muslin wheel with blue rouge on the flex shaft or with a polishing cloth.

Broken Chain?

Don't panic! This pattern is one that can be fixed without soldering it or taking it apart. There will likely be only one wire sticking out. If so, with the scriber, open up a small space between links, where the loose wire came out, and push the loose end into it. Use very fine round or chain nose pliers to close the links around it. Once the surrounding links are closed around the loose end, it won't work its way back out. The double woven chain prevents one broken link from making the chain fall apart.

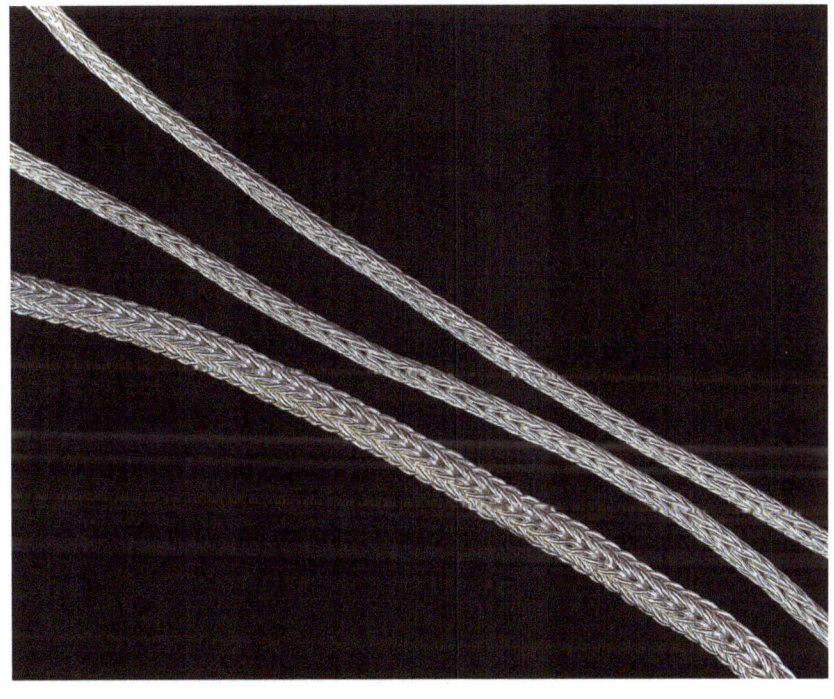

2-Directional Double-Weave chains
Top: 24 gauge wire, 10mm mandrel
Middle: 22 gauge wire, 11mm mandrel
Bottom: by Pete Macko, 20 gauge wire, 12mm mandrel

End Caps

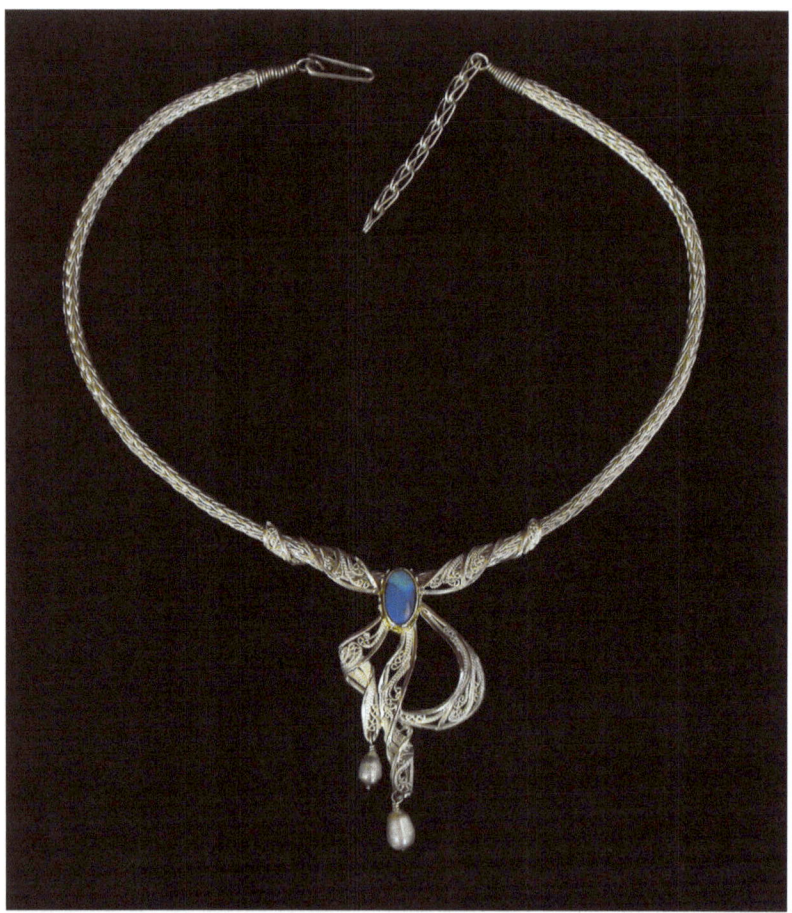

The multidirectional chains have loose ends that must be wrapped up or covered. Many styles of commercial end caps are available, but being able to make your own expands your design options and allows you to create ones that relate to your overall composition.

End caps can be constructed out of sheet or wrapped from wire. They can be cylinders, or they can be tapered. The wrapped end caps on *Entwine* IV (left) are tapered and create a transition from the 2-Directional Double-Weave chain to the 2" of 1-Direction Single-Weave chain that serves to make the necklace adjustable.

Entwine IV

Russian filigree, granulation, and 2-Directional Double-Weave necklace; Sterling silver, fine silver, 18k, 22k gold, Lightning Ridge opal, Biwa pearls, pendant: 3" long x 3" wide x 1/4" deep, 18" adjustable chain; 2008

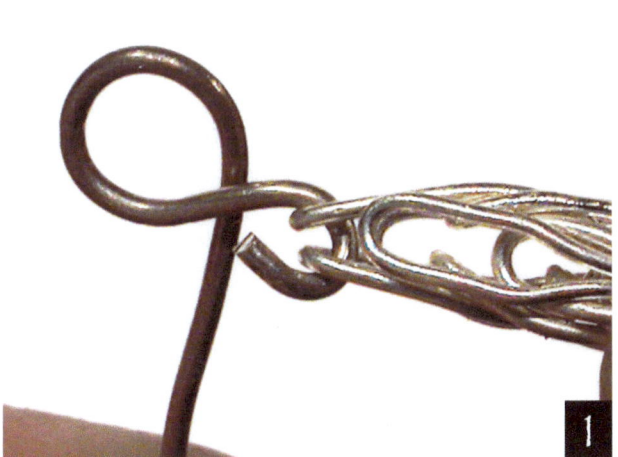

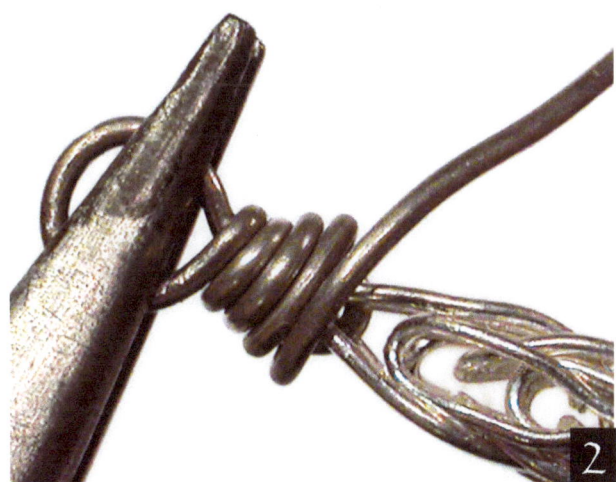

Wrapped End Caps

1 Use 20 gauge sterling silver round wire to make an asymmetrical figure eight, beginning with the small side of the figure eight. The larger side of the figure eight will serve as a jump ring, so make it more circular. Hook the smaller side through the two loops of the last link of the chain. Close it with pliers.

2 Begin wrapping the wire around the middle of the figure eight, making each wrap slightly larger in diameter. It may be easier to hold the wire and the jump ring with pliers. Take care that the wraps are completely even and parallel to each other and that there are no gaps between them.

3 Wrap a few more times past the two final links. Cut the wire, and bend the tip of it 90 degrees inward.

4 Use the scriber to open a space between

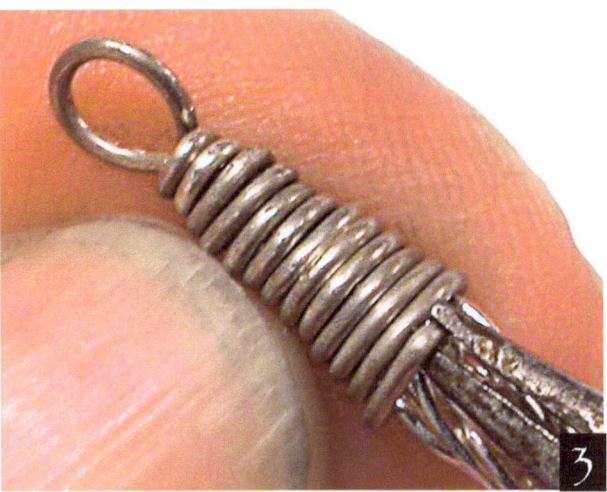

links, and push the bent tip of the wire into the space. Repeat the process for the other end of the chain, taking care to make it match the first. Make a basic clasp (page 23) and attach it to the jump ring of one wrapped end. You can also wrap with two strands of 22 gauge sterling silver wire that have been twisted together to create a different look.

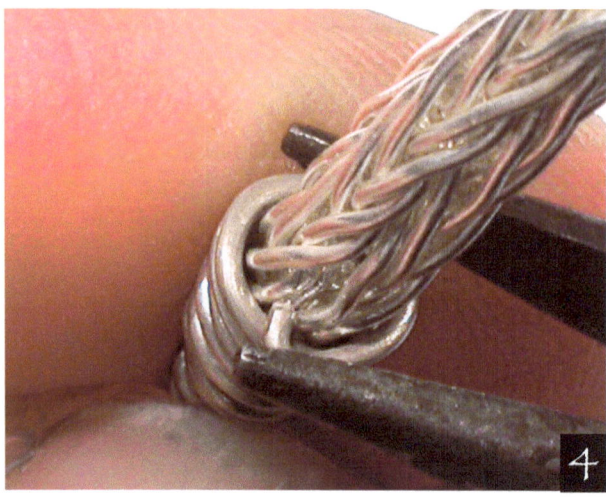

Constructed End Caps

In the interest of clarity, these directions are for making one end cap. Repeat the process for the second one, or make them both at one time. The sheet can be stamped or roller printed prior to construction.

Bend a 1/2" strip of 24 gauge sterling sheet around the chain, and mark where it meets as you would a bezel. Cut the sheet where it is marked, and file the edges straight. Close the tube, and solder the seam with hard solder. The tube does not have to be perfectly shaped when it is soldered. The edges just have to meet. Once soldered, shape the tube over a bezel mandrel or a dapping punch to make it round. Solder the tube to another piece of sheet with hard solder.

Soldering the edge of a jump ring to a sheet is not a secure joint because there is not enough surface contact between the edge of round wire and the flat sheet. To make the joint more secure, drill a hole just big enough to accommodate 20 gauge round wire in the center of the capped end. Make a jump ring from 20 gauge sterling silver round wire, but instead of cutting it to form only a circle, leave a 1/4" tail of wire, bent at a 90 degree angle to the circle. Insert the tail into the hole in the end cap, and solder it from the top with medium solder so that the end of the circle is soldered closed and soldered to the end cap as well.

Sweat solder them to the chain by flowing easy solder inside the end cap or by coating the inside with easy paste solder. Insert the chain, and heat the end

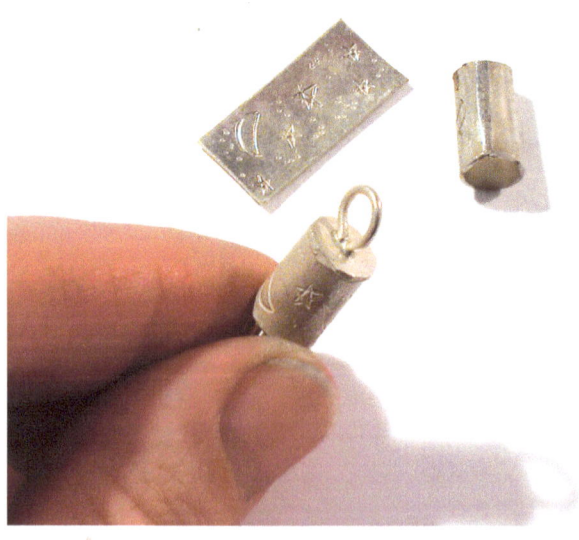

Examples of the stages of constructing an end cap from sheet

cap with the torch. The heat will be conducted to the chain within, and the solder will flow to join it to the tube. (Because the chain will not conduct much heat away from the end cap, there is no reason to heat all of it.) Make sure the jump rings on the end caps lay parallel to each other so that the chain will not twist when worn.

Another alternative is to solder flat wire across the top of the end cap before bending it into a clasp such as in the piece *Occulto* III (below). The other end cap of the chain has a clasp that has been pinched permanently closed.

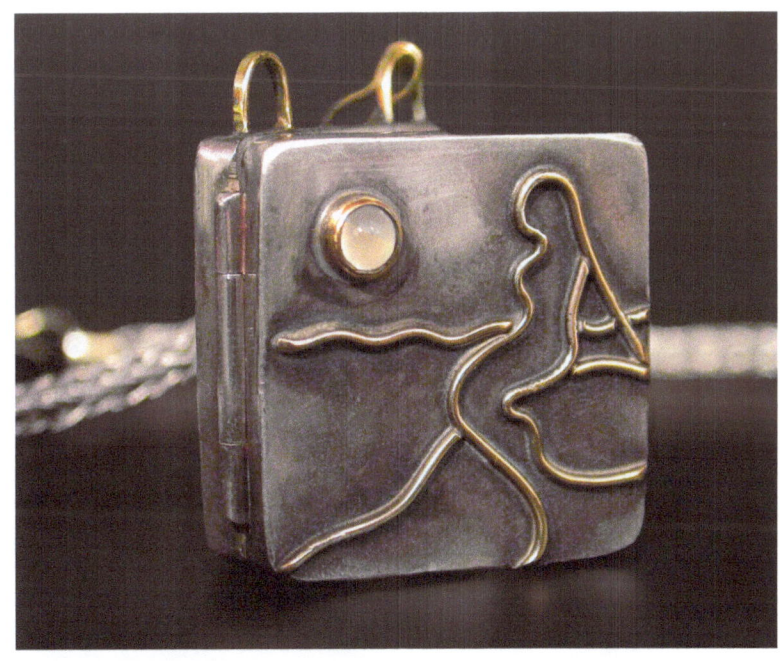

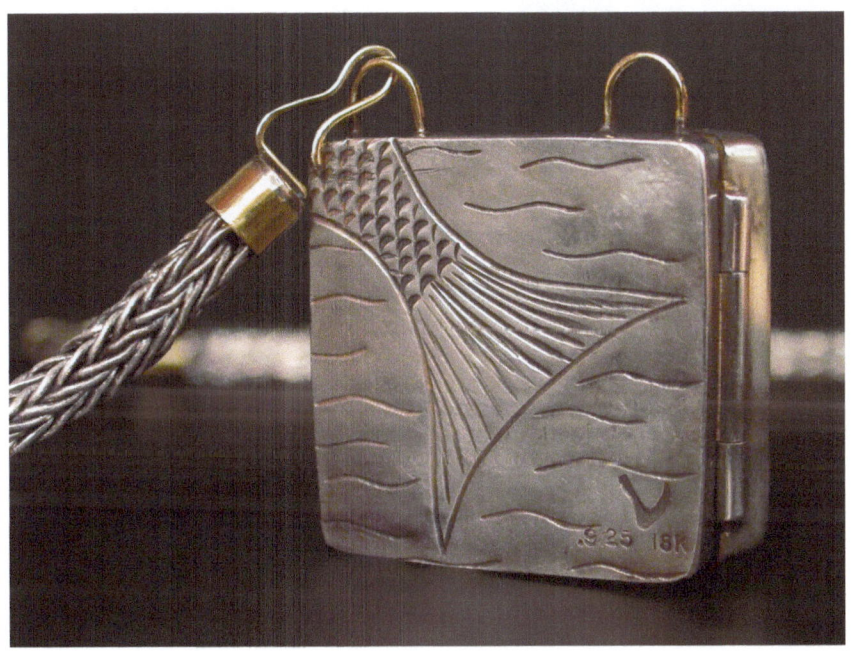

Occulto III

Chased, wire granulation locket on a 2-Directional Double-Weave chain; sterling silver, fine silver, 18k, 22k , gold, moonstone: 1-3/8" long x 1-3/8" wide x 3/8" deep, 18" chain; 2004

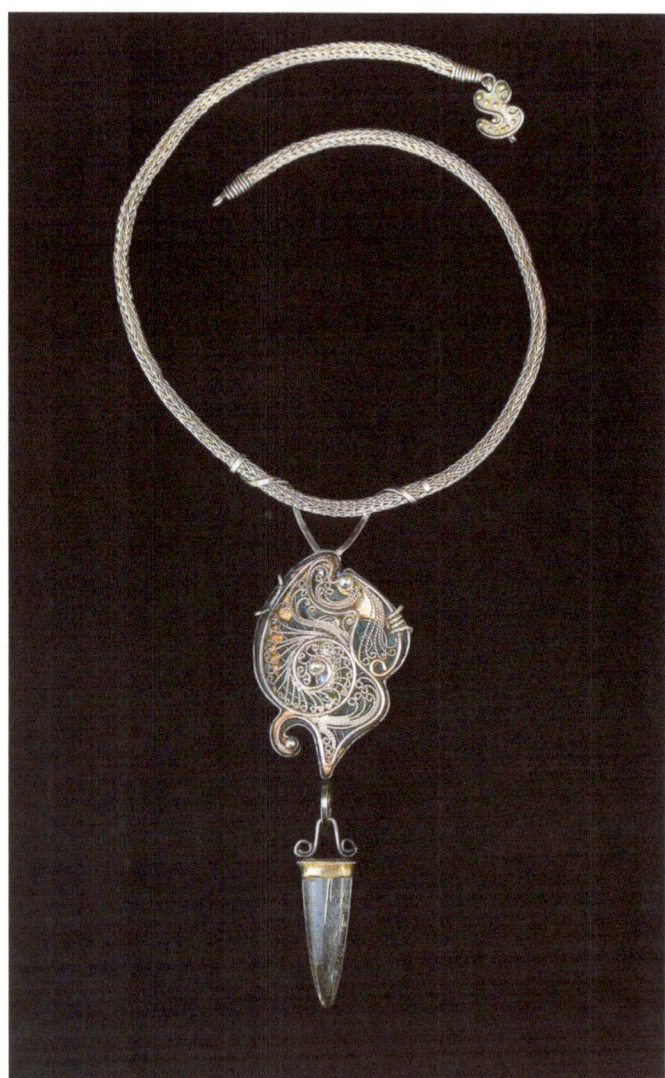

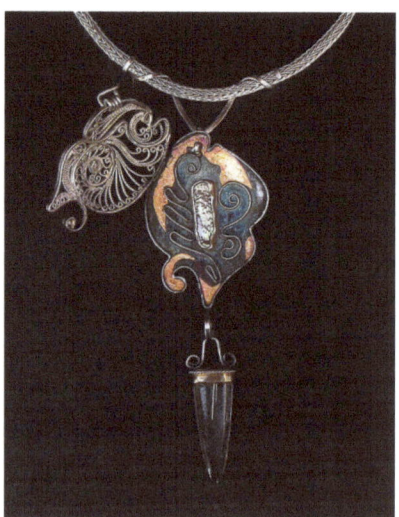

Pearls of Wisdom

Russian filigree, granulation, and kum boo amulet 2-Directional Double-Weave chain; 22k, 24k gold, fine silver, sterling silver, Baroque pearl, rutilated quartz; 3" long x 1-1/2" wide; 2000

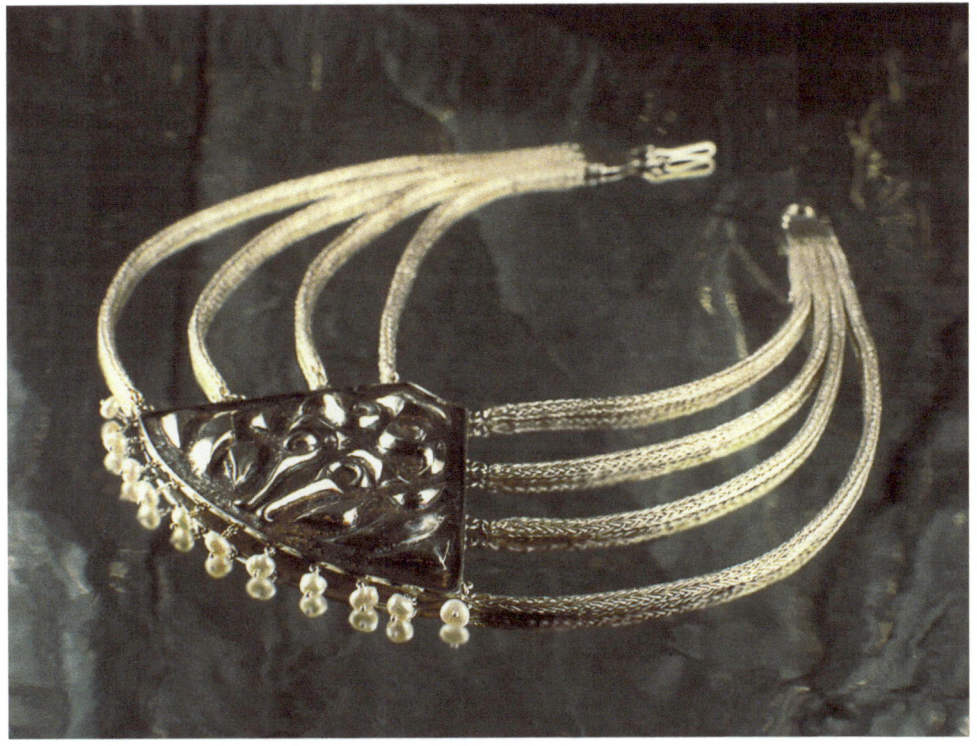

Eastern Calligraphy X

High relief Eastern repoussé and 2-Directional Double-Weave necklace; fine silver, sterling silver, 7" outside diameter; 1995; photo: Jennifer Clifton

3-Directional Single-Weave

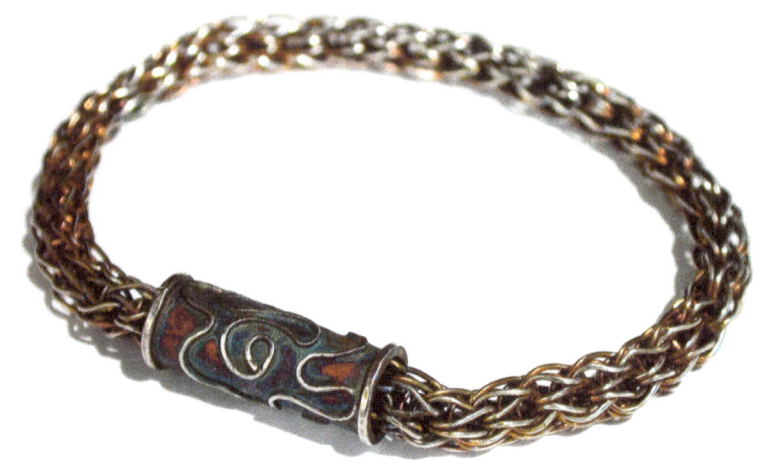

Organic Interconnection VIII

3-Directional Single-Weave and wire granulation bracelet; sterling silver, fine

slver; 3/8" thick, 2-3/4" in diameter; 2008

Ancient multidirectional chains are sometimes woven from 3 and even 4 directions. Gorgeous as they can be, from a practical standpoint, if I want a larger diameter double-weave chain, I usually use larger mandrels and gauges of wire. The 3-Directional Single-Weave chain, however, is an exception. There are pieces that just seem to call for this unique round chain.

This chain weaves as a triangle and gets stretched or very lightly hammered round. The links are woven through only one set of loops (one link) at a time. When in doubt where to weave, always look for the two open loops that sit lowest of the six on top.

The unique depth of the chain can be accentuated by patination. After the piece is complete, patina with liver of sulphur or Jax Silver Blackener™. For a Medieval feel, take the patina off the surface with a ScotchBrite™ pad to matte the outside edges of the links, leaving the inside dark. For a shinier effect, rub the outside of the patinated chain with a SparkleSparkle Ultracloth™ which will leave the outside edges high polished and the inside dark.

Metal & Mandrel

22 gauge fine silver round wire,
   1.25 to 1.5 oz for a 7" bracelet

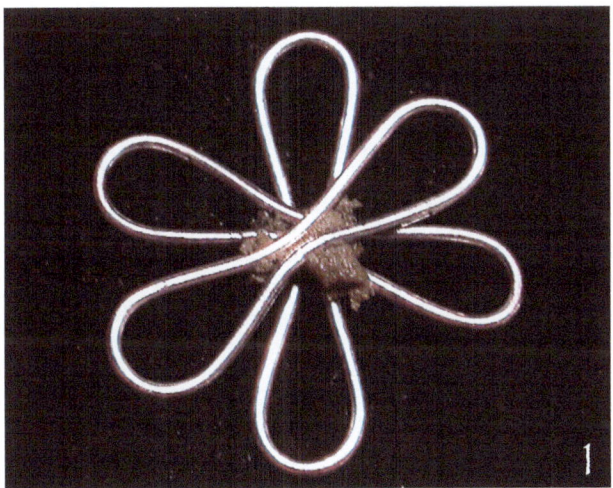

1 Form the three links that you set aside so they are more open and symmetrical. Solder them together with easy paste or other type solder in the shape of what I call a "70's flower."

2 Bend the loops straight up. Because this starter link can be difficult to hold, make a handle for it by twisting a piece of wire onto the bottom of it as shown on page 45.

Weave a link straight through the set of loops that sits the lowest (the bottom link). Bend the link into a "U" shape, but do not pinch it closed. Weave another link through the two open loops that now sit the lowest and bend it into a "U". Repeat the step to weave a link through the loops of the third direction.

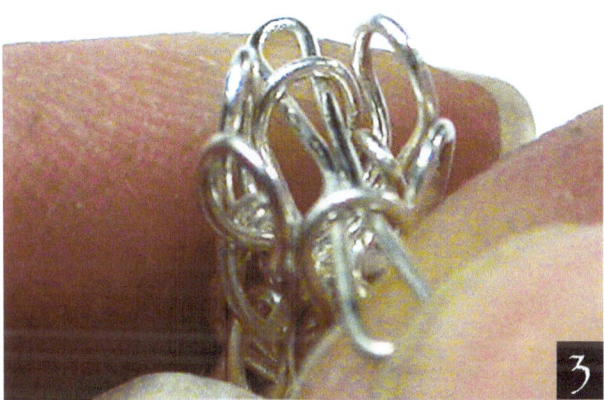

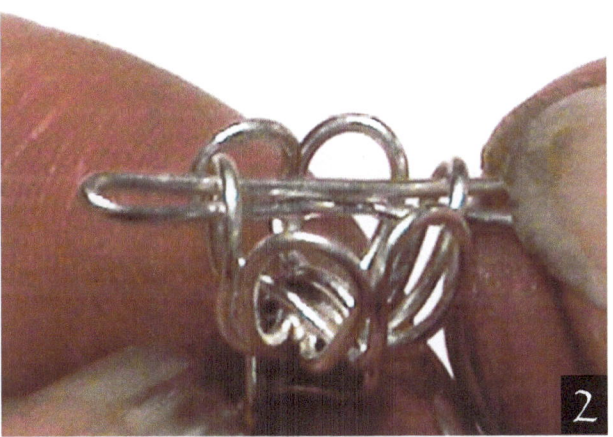

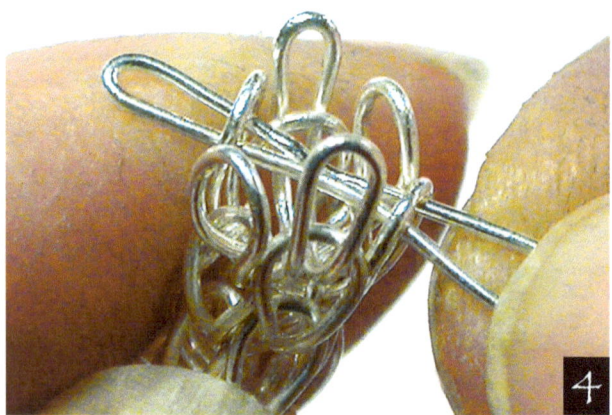

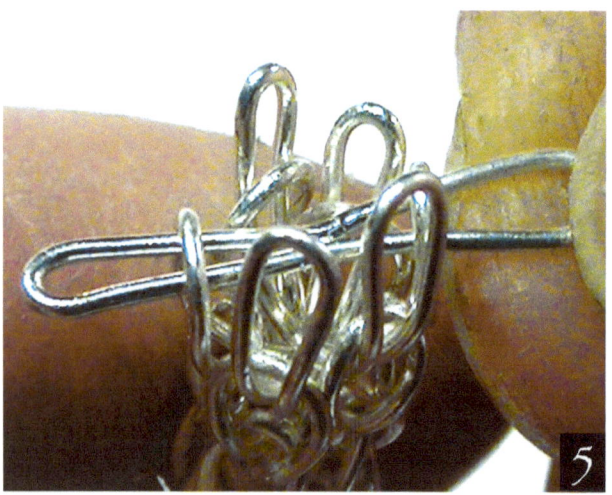

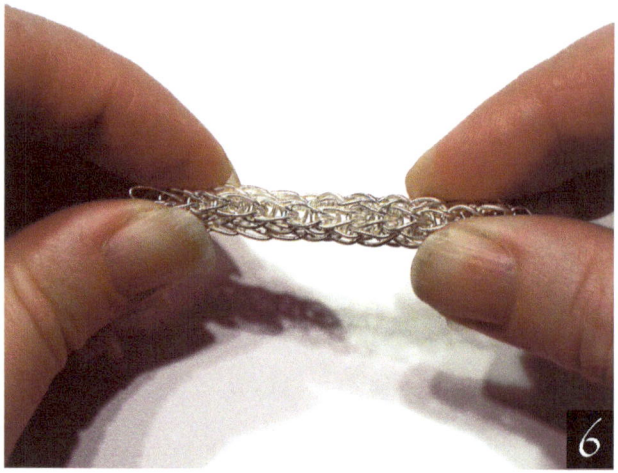

6 At any point when there is enough chain to hold onto, grasp the chain at each end and pull. Stretching will help round the chain without squashing it. If it still needs rounding or compressing, hammer it lightly with a rawhide mallet as directed on page 46. Take care not to stretch or hammer too much. It can't be decompressed! Finish the ends with constructed or wrapped end caps.

3-5 Continue weaving links in the three directions, using a scriber to open up the links as needed.

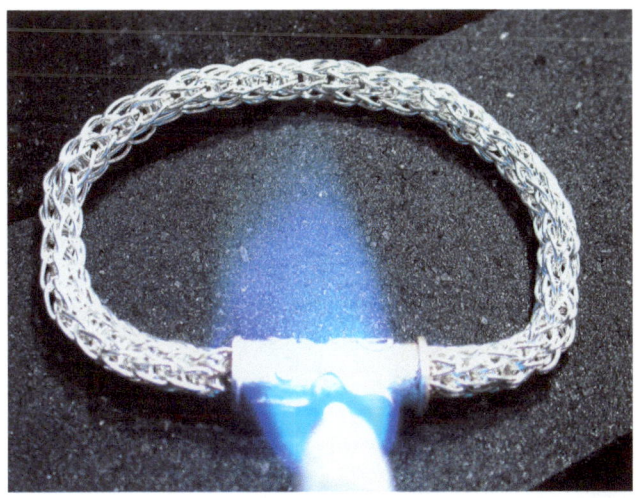

Organic Interconnection VIII (page 54) is a flexible bangle. Both ends of the chain are soldered into the wire granulation bead in the same manner as the end caps described in the End Caps chapter (page 48).

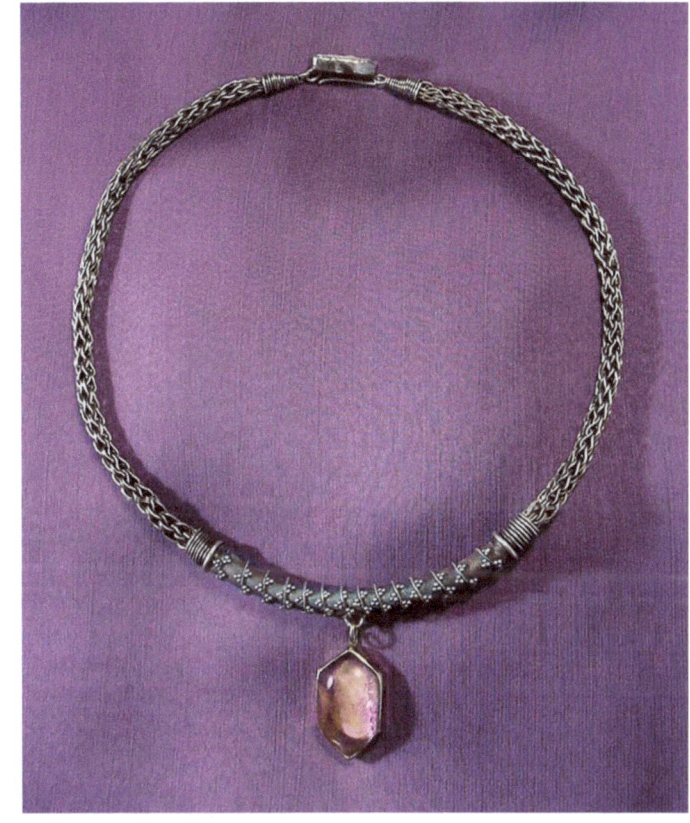

Talisman for Serenity

Granulation and 3-Directional Single-Weave necklace; sterling silver, fine silver, ametrine 8" in diameter; 2000

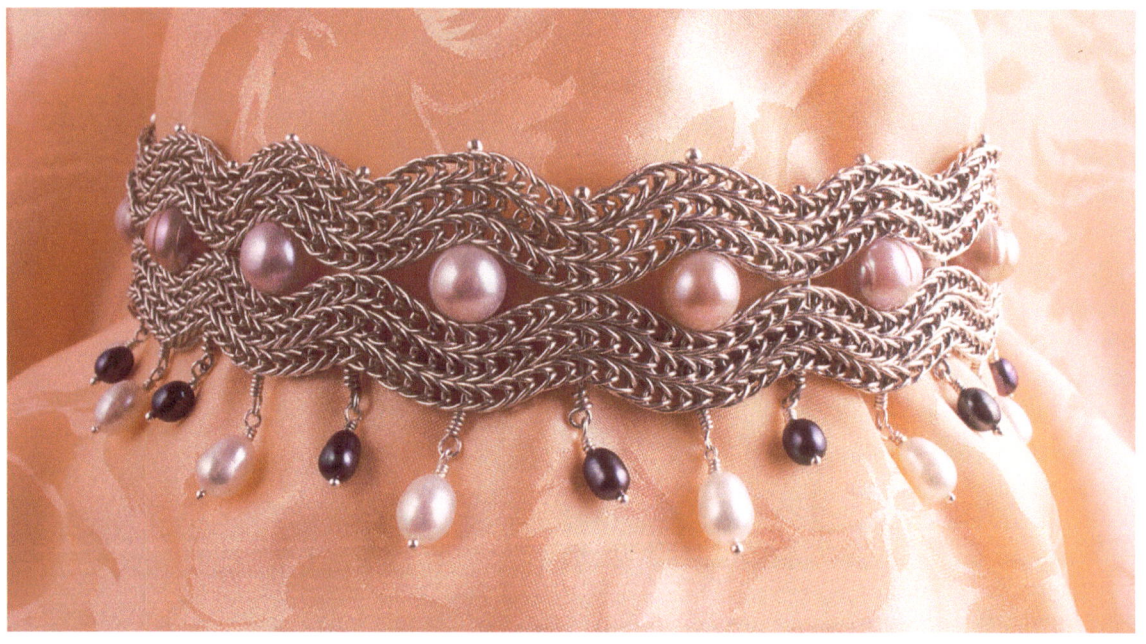

"Amidst the Lantern Light II

Undulating Mesh choker; fine silver, sterling silver, Biwa and freshwater pearls; 2" wide, adjustable to 16" long; 1996

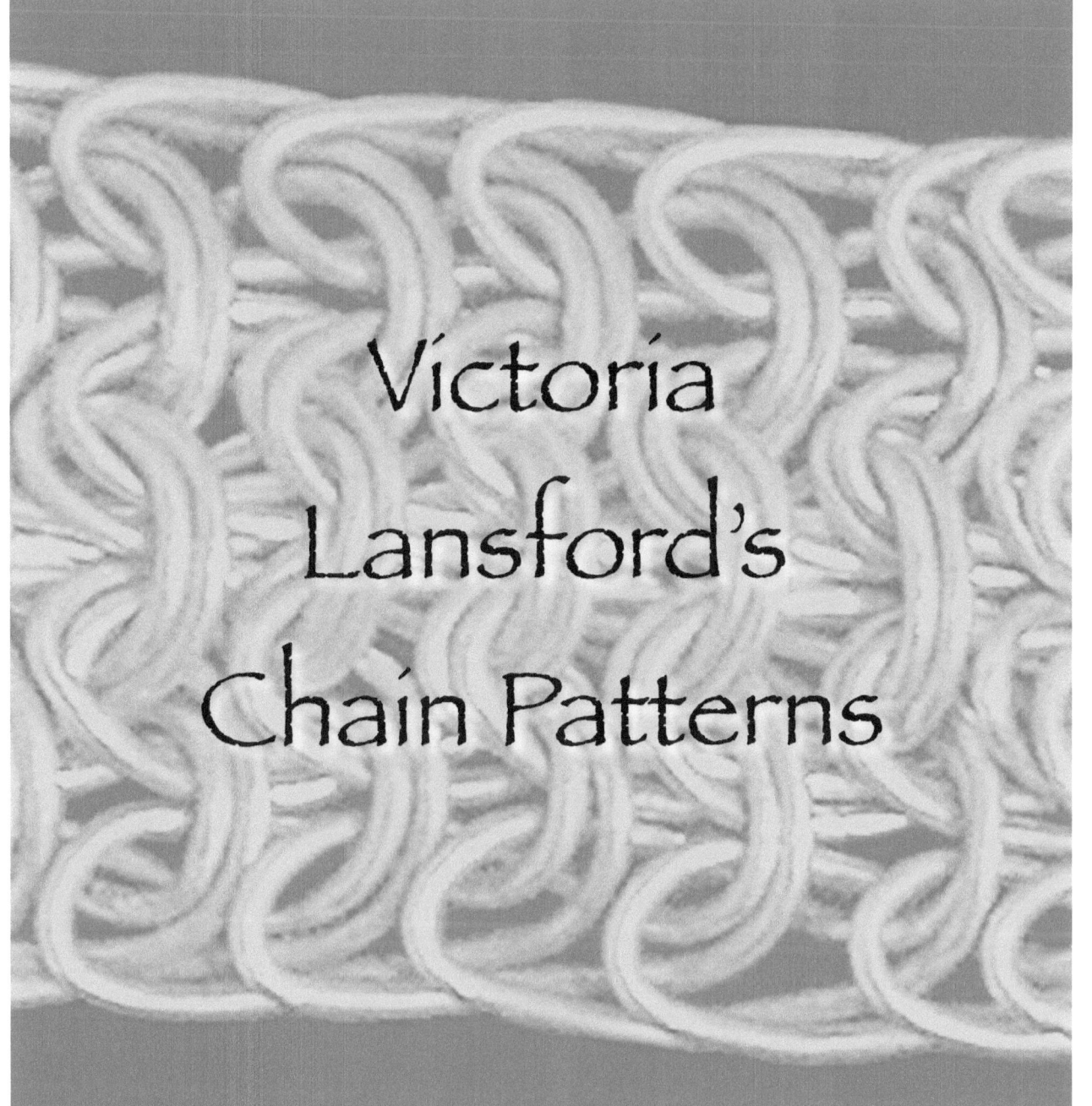

Victoria Lansford's Chain Patterns

Undulating Mesh Chain

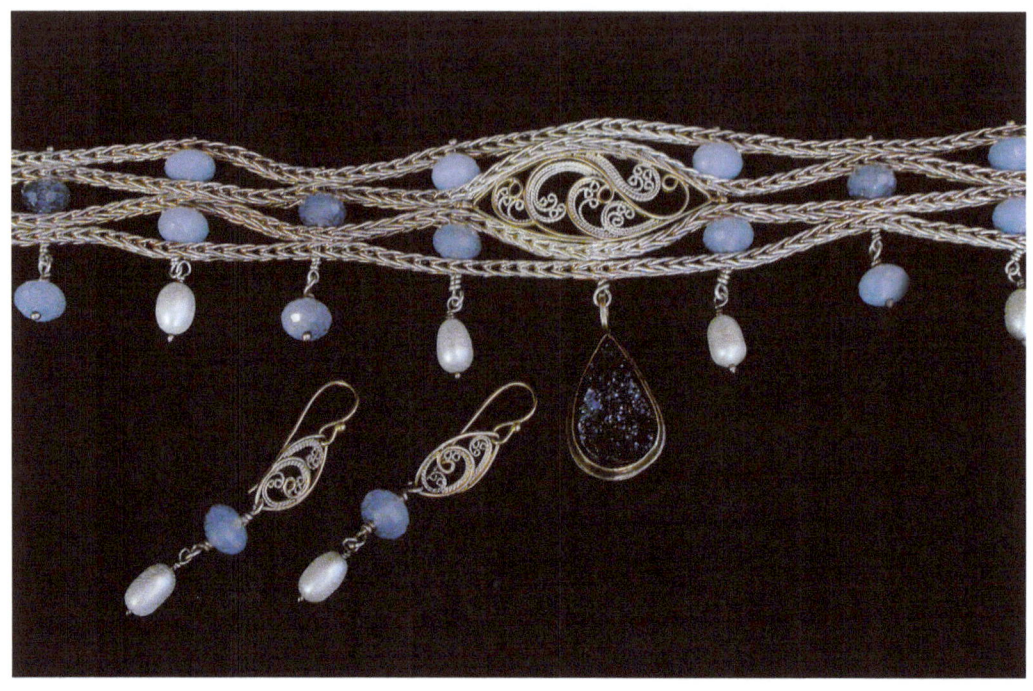

Eye of the Beholder
Russian filigree and undulating mesh choker and earrings; sterling silver, fine silver, 18k, 22k gold, titanium bonded chalcedony drusy, chalcedony, Biwa pearls; 2-1/2" wide at center, adjustable

The Undulating Mesh chain is composed of multiple 1-Direction Double-Weave chains (page 36) connected by wrap ties and dangles (page 30). If making a choker, a mesh that is tapered at the back can be more comfortable to wear than one that is wide all the way around the neck. Bracelets can be the same width all the way around.

Metal & Mandrel
22 gauge fine silver round wire, 2-4 oz, depending on the width and length of the finished piece, plus extra for dangles

20 gauge fine silver for connecting wrap ties

10mm or 11mm mandrel

Beads or pearls

Forming the links

For all but the links that finish off the ends and make the chain adjustable, follow steps 1-3 of the 1-Direction Double-Weave pattern (page 36).

Decide how wide you would like your chain. The one pictured uses four separate 1-Direction Double-weave chains. The mesh will work with only two or three chains, but I recommend learning with four because the options for incorporating beads and other elements are more intuitive.

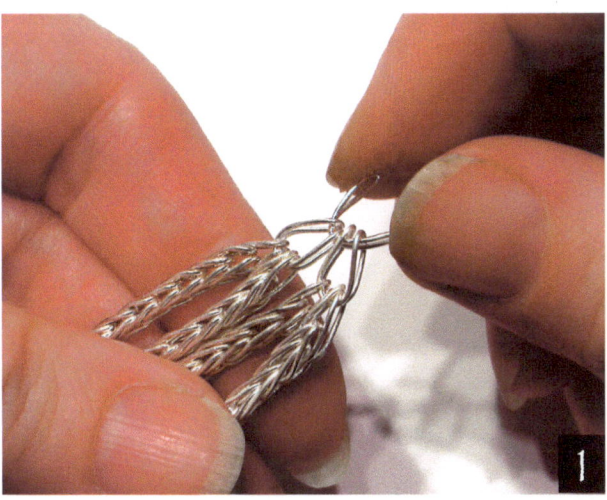

1 Following the directions for the 1-Direction Double-Weave chain (page 36), weave two to three inches of four different 1-Direction Double-Weave chains (hereafter referred to as 1DDW for short). Lay two of the 1DDW chains parallel to each other so that the first links line up loop facing loop. Weave a link through all four of these loops, and pinch it closed.

Repeat this step for the other two 1DDW chains. Repeat the step again to join all four chains together as pictured. Be sure to pinch the final one closed tightly, so that it will not fall out as you continue weaving the working ends of the 1DDW chains.

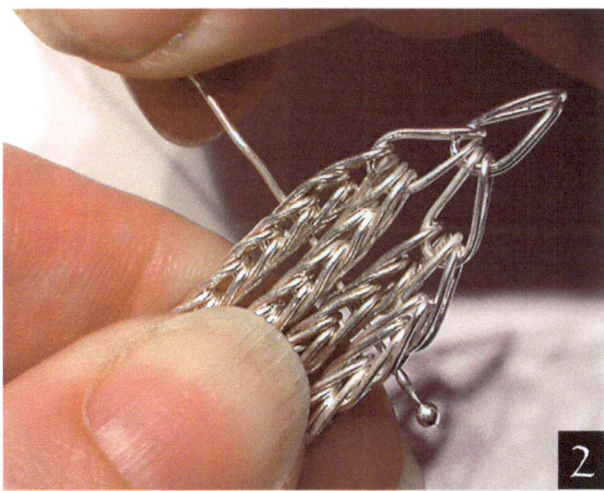

2 Make head pins (page 31) with the 20 gauge fine silver round wire. The balled up ends should be large enough not to slip through the 1DDW chains but not so large that they stick up above the chain too far. Balls that stick up too far can be uncomfortable when the chain is worn.

Looking at the side of one of the outside 1DDW chains, count five links from the end (not from the final unifying links). Insert a head pin into the hole of this fifth link, continuing straight through of all four 1DDW chains and out the side of the last chain.

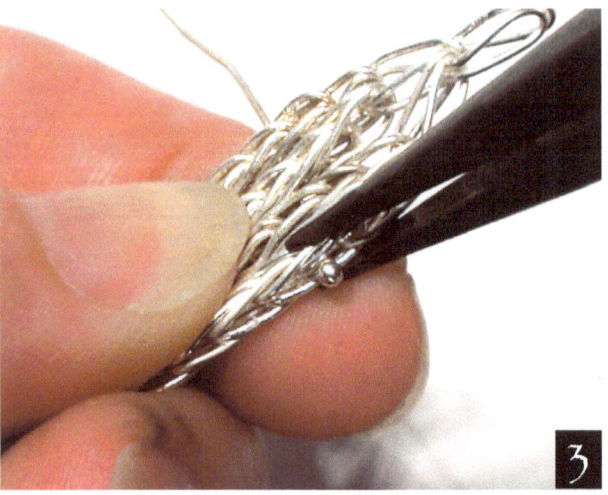

the wrap tie is tight enough to hold the 1DDW chains close together.

4 Count five links down from the head pin. Insert another head pin through the hole in this fifth link. Before sliding the head pin through all the 1DDW chains, divide them in the middle so that there are two chains on the left and two on the right. Place a bead in between with the drill holes lined up next to the chains. Now insert the head pin through all four 1DDW chains and the bead in the middle. Finish off with another loop and wrap tie.

3 You may need to open up a small space with your scriber. If the hole is too big, and the ball slips through, use fine chain nose pliers to squish it more closed. Ideally the ball should only stick up about halfway above the side of the chain. finish off the other end of the head pin with a loop and a wrap tie (page 31). Make sure

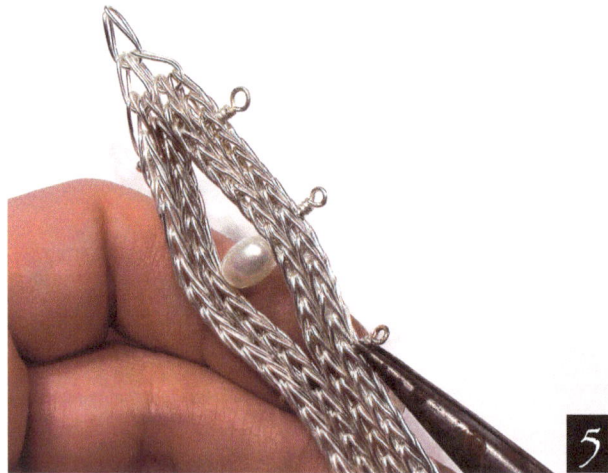

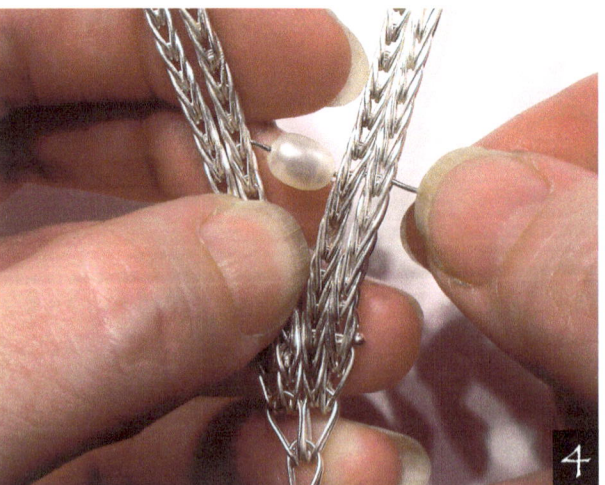

5 Repeat steps 3-4 with beads on alternating head pins. For a choker, keep all the wrap ties on one side of the mesh. For a bracelet, you can keep them on the same side, alternate sides, or finish with wrap ties both sides, wherever you would like to have dangles Continue weaving the 1DDW chains two to three inches at a time and adding head pins to join them until the mesh is within one to two inches of the desired total length. (The finishing links and clasp will add more length.)

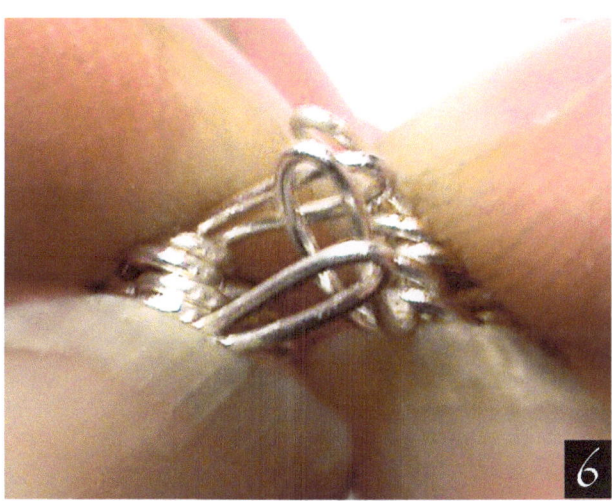

6 To end the mesh, cross the last links of the two 1DDW chains on the left as shown and weave a link through all four loops.

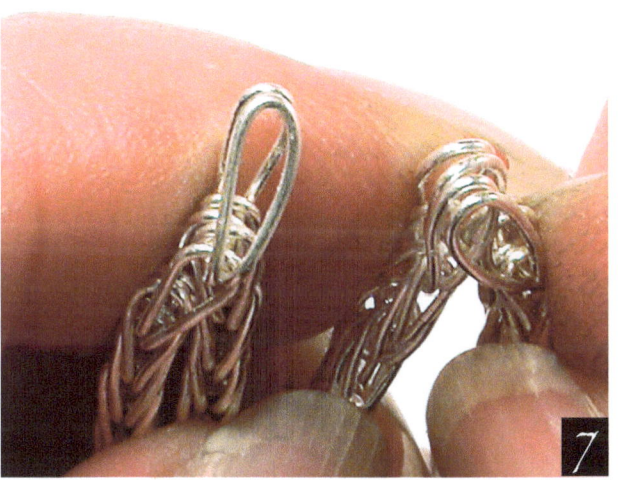

7 Repeat step 6 for the two other chains.

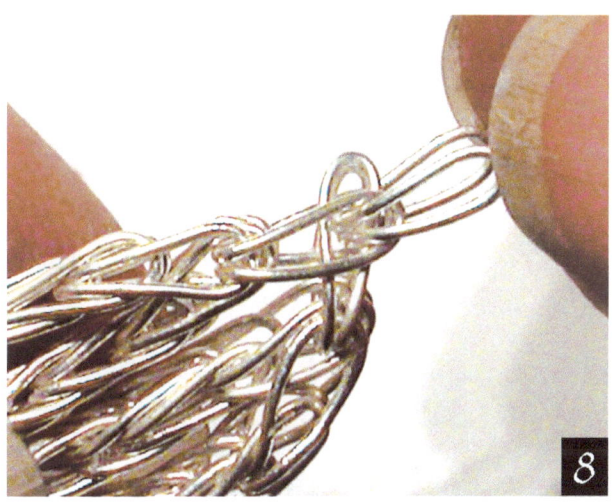

8 Repeat step 6 again to join the remaining links. At one end of the mesh attach a basic clasp (page 23) to this last link.

At the other end of the mesh from the last link, weave two more inches of links in the 1-Direction Single-Weave pattern. Solder together the loops of the last link so that it cannot come loose from the chain. This tail of chain will make the mesh adjustable, and the basic clasp can hook anywhere into it.

Attach dangles (page 30) to the wrap tie ends of the head pins. For chokers 22 gauge fine silver round wire is adequate. For bracelets use 20 gauge. If using pearls, you may need to redrill the holes to accommodate the wire. Use a regular drill bit the size of your wire. Drill slowly so that the pearls do not become damaged from overheating.

Vertebrate Chain

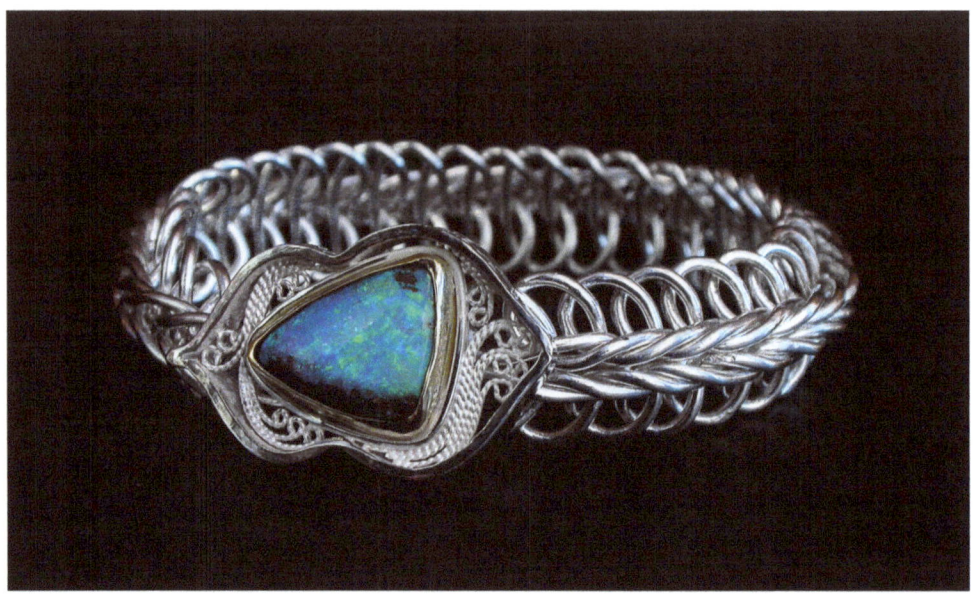

From the series, Vertebracelet, Vertebrate pattern bracelet with Russian filigree clasp; sterling silver, fine silver, 22k gold, Koroit opal; 8" long x 5/8" wide; 2008

The Vertebrate pattern was the first chain pattern I invented. The name comes from the spiny look of the chain's back. The pattern is somewhat reminiscent of an ancient one called a side weave, which has a braid motif down the center of one side; however, the Vertebrate is much more three dimensional. The tight braid forms because the chain is a double weave pattern, meaning each link is woven through two previous links at a time.

Because the links are formed by hand without the use of pliers, vertebrates by different people are often as unique as handwriting. The goal is uniformity in one's own links and not necessarily in making them look exactly like someone else's. If, after weaving them together, they don't look at all even, take heart! There are steps devoted to truing up even the most wavering chains. The vertebrate is surprisingly fast and remains many of my students' favorite.

The chain can be polished with a SparkleSparkle Ultracloth™ or blue rouge on a mini muslin wheel on the flex shaft.

Metal & Mandrel

16 gauge fine silver round wire, 1.5 ounces for a 7" bracelet

19mm mandrel

4" 18 gauge sterling round wire

Metal and/or stone for clasp top (optional)

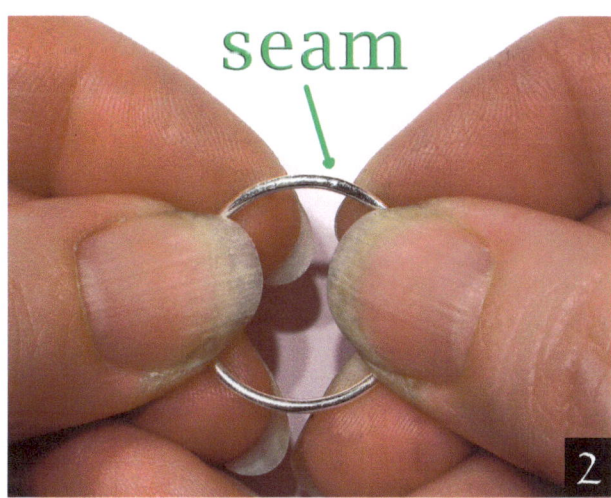

2 Hold a link between your thumbs and first two fingers as shown. Make sure the seam is at the 1 o'clock position. Bend the link by pushing your thumbs into the space between your index and middle fingers, curving the link downward at the 3 o'clock and 6 o'clock positions.

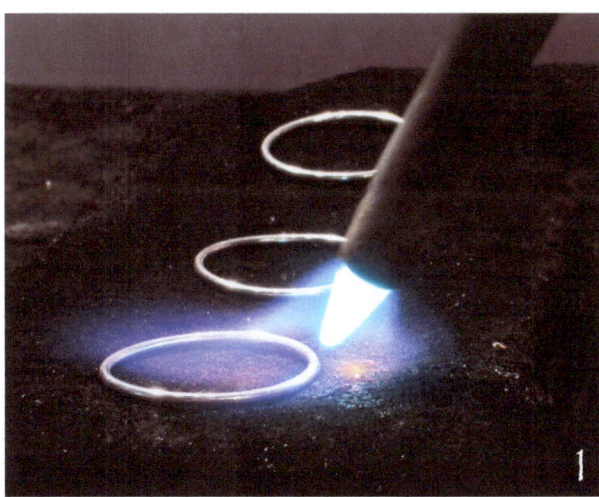

1 The process for fusing 16 gauge links is the same as for the other patterns in the book (page 12). Some people find that fusing 16 gauge is easier than fusing smaller gauges. Unfortunately, bigger isn't always better since any mistakes, blobs, or thin areas are highly visible. Links that have thin spots are too vulnerable to use (see page 15). The normal reticulation (rough surface) around the seam ends up on the back of the chain and is mostly burnished away in the weaving process. Yes, you can cut 16 gauge wire with Joyce Chen™ scissors!

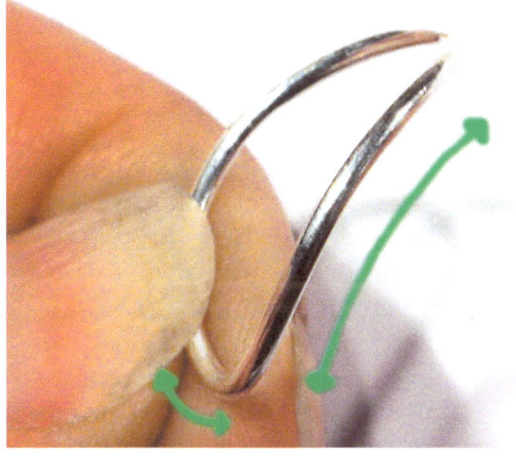

View of of the saddle shaped curves created in step 2

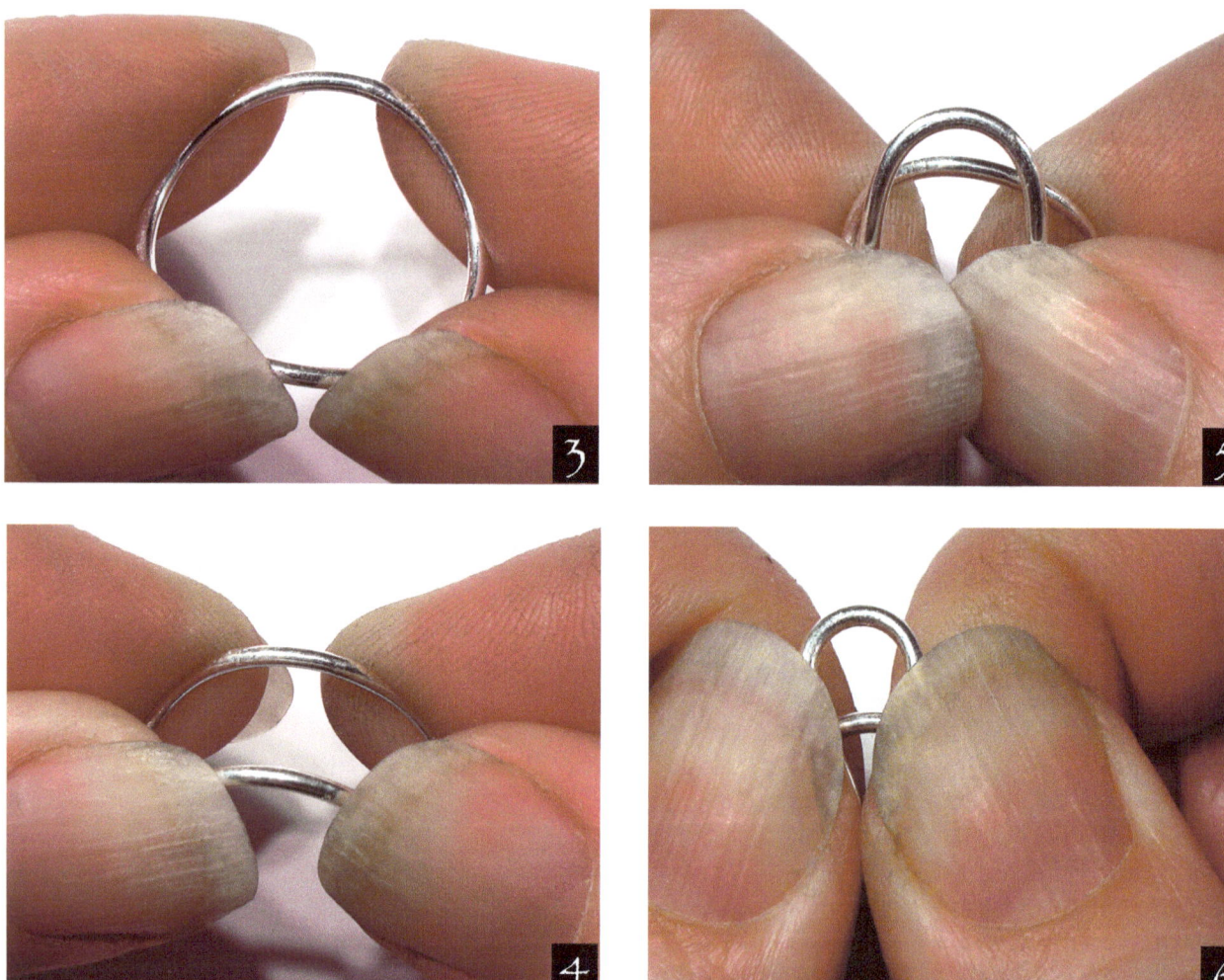

3-4 Change your grasp of the link so that it sits between your thumbs and index fingers. Push your thumbs forward and at the same time pull your index fingers back. The link will begin to fold in half like a taco shell, but the pressure of your thumbs going forward will push one half beyond the other.

5-6 As you continue pushing the front half beyond the back half, bring your thumbs together to push the front half together at the bottom. Your index fingers will hold the other half in a semi circle. Leave space between the front and back halves.

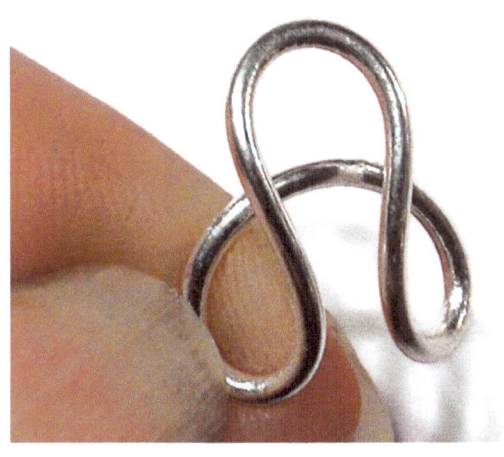

View of the link when beginning to bring thumbs together in step 5

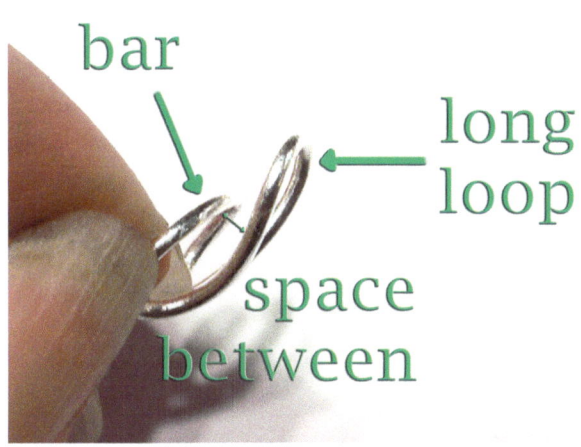

Anatomy of a formed link. Note the space left between the front and back portions of the link.

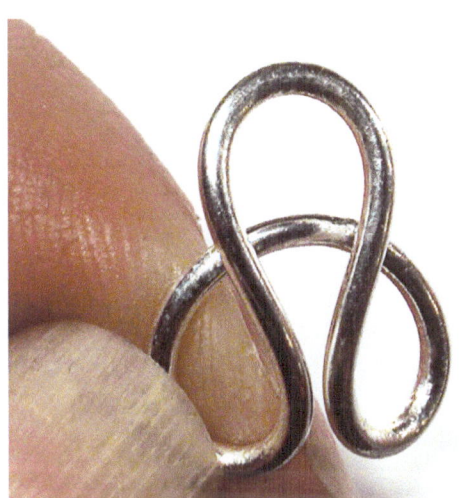

View of the link after bringing thumbs together in step 6

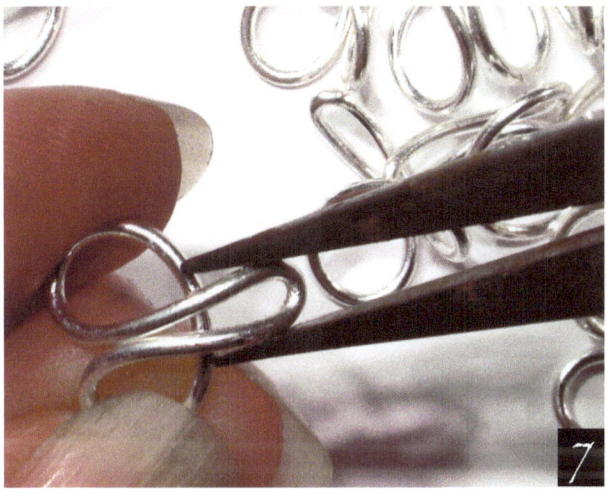

7 Set aside one link. Use chain nose pliers to pinch the long loop on all the other links, taking care *not* to pinch them all the way closed.

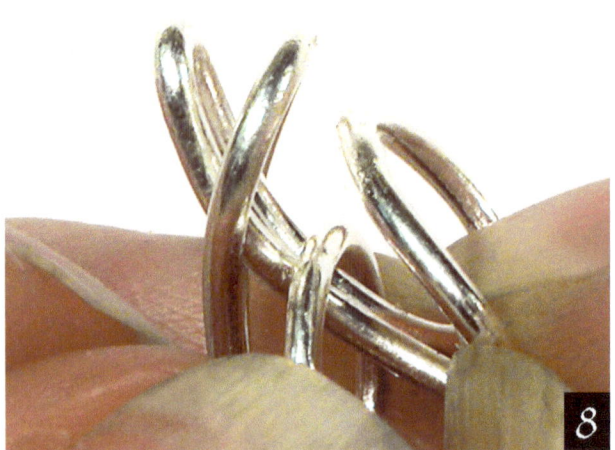

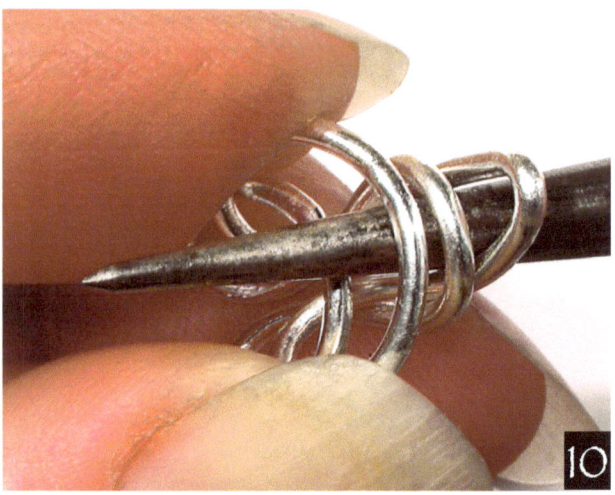

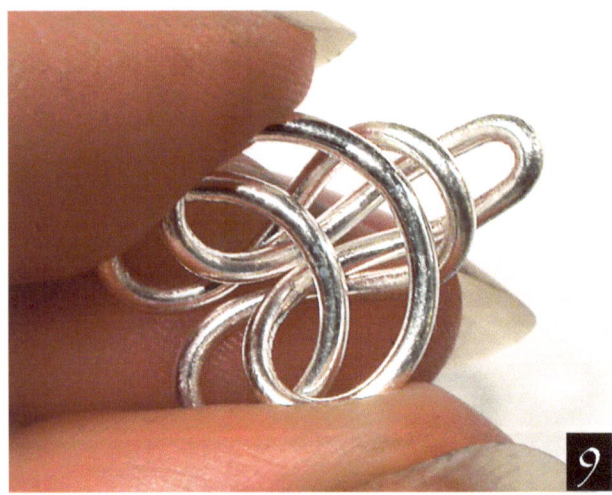

the new link will slide over the bar but not past the long loop of the first link.

10 From the underside, insert a scriber though both long loops and the closest bar.

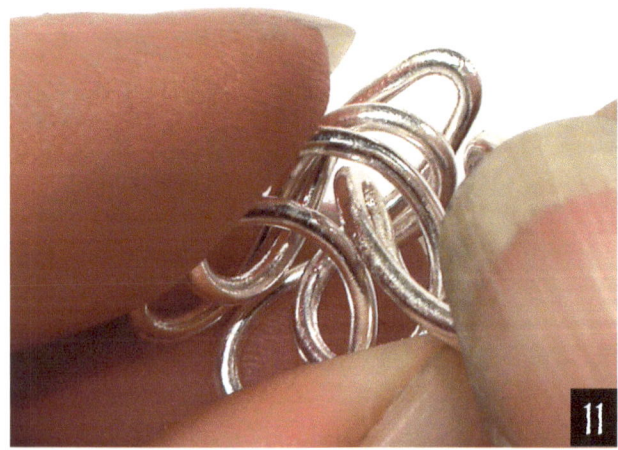

8-9 This chain is woven from the back. The braid pattern will appear on the underside (which is actually the chain's front).

    Hold the unpinched link that you set aside so that the bar is face up. Weave the long loop of a pinched link through the bar and long loop of the first link. The bar of

11 Weave a link through the last bar and both long loops.

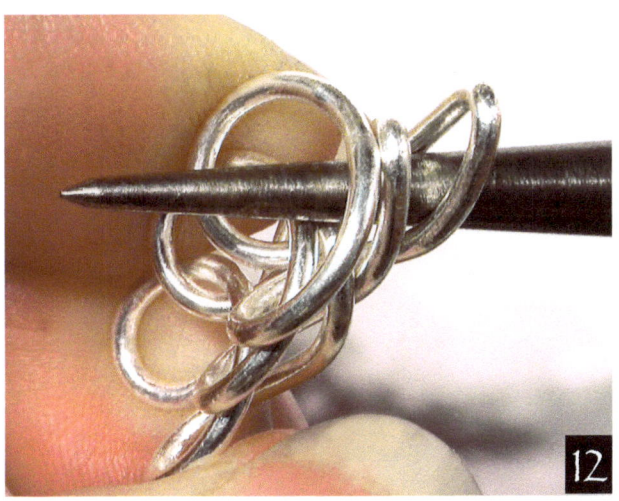

Repeat steps 10-12 until the chain is the desired length. If making a bracelet, it should be just long enough to wrap around your wrist. The clasp will create enough slack for the bracelet to be comfortable.

After weaving a few links, you will notice that the chain naturally curves backwards, with the bars on the outside. To make it curve so that the braid is on the outside instead, bend over your thumbs a few links at a time.

If your chain looks open and uneven, don't worry! There are several more steps left that will dramatically improve it.

12 Now insert the scriber through the last two long loops and the last bar, which will be through the second and third links. Remove the scriber, and weave a link through the last bar and last two long loops.

Always insert the scriber from the underside, but weave links from the side with the bars on top (the back). From the third row on, each link is woven through the previous two links or through *one bar and two long loops* (your new mantra).

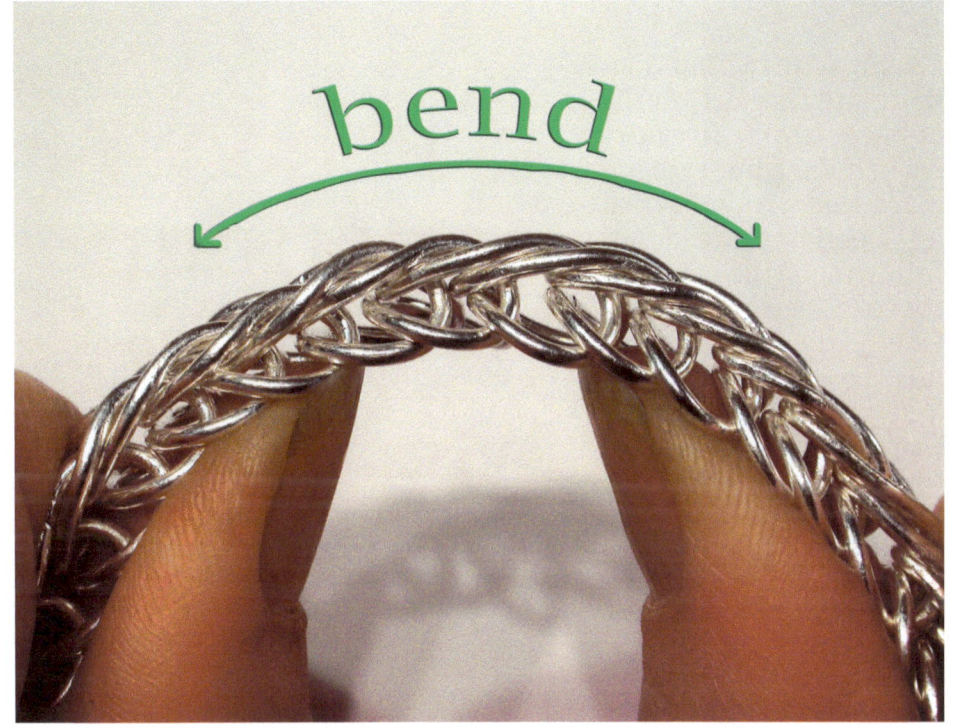

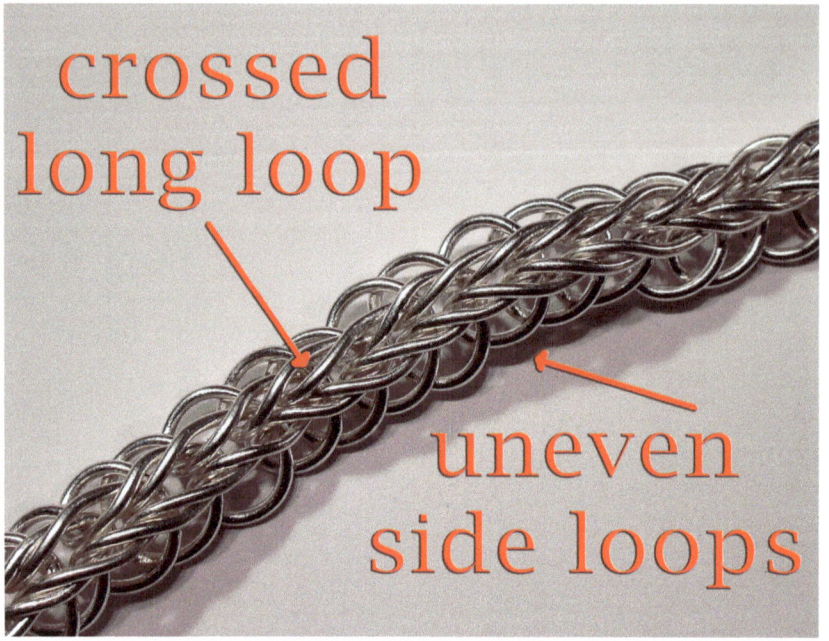

crossed
long loop

uneven
side loops

13 You may find that there are "breaks" in the curve, not literally broken links but rather a place that bends back at an angle instead of following the forced curve. These are places where the bar of one link lays past the long loop of the next link. Use a scriber as shown to push the bar back into place.

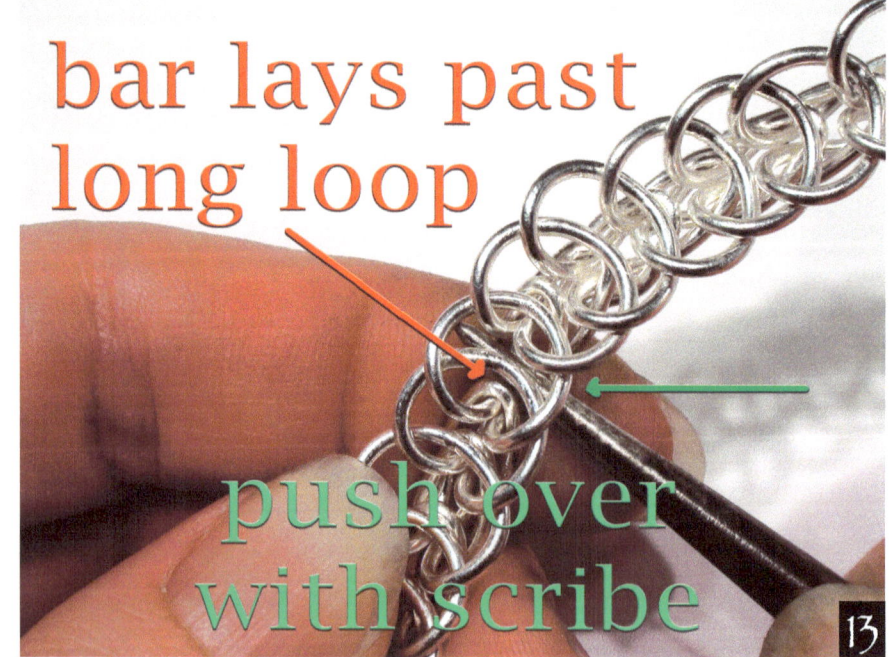

bar lays past
long loop

push over
with scribe

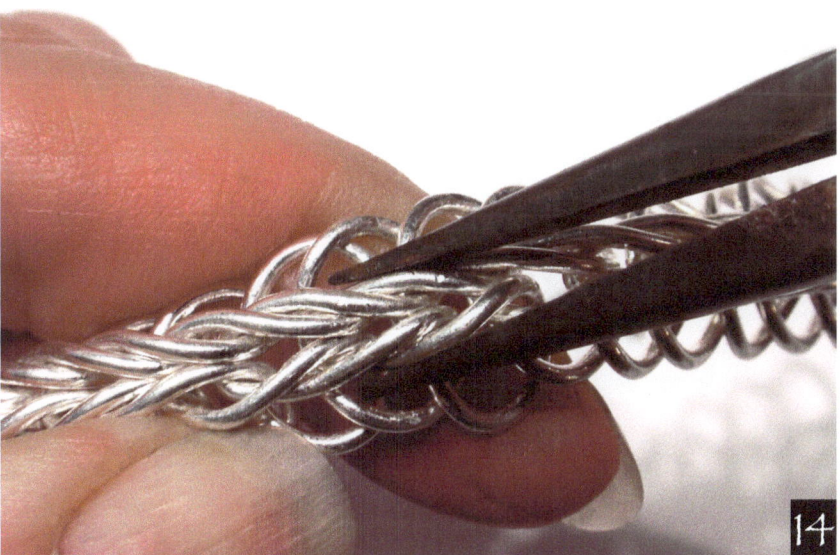

14 Use chain nose pliers to pinch the long loops and tighten the braid on the top. Take care not to let the sides of the long loops, which form the braid, cross over each other.

15 Use round pliers to pull open the side loops. For links that are uneven, pull harder on one side so that the outside edges of the side loops are in line with each other.

This step will spread the braid slightly open so repeat step 13 to tighten it up again. While it may seem counterintuitive to pinch the braid first, the chain will be more even and properly work hardened if you pinch before and after opening the side loops. Steps 13-14 can be repeated as needed until the chain is even.

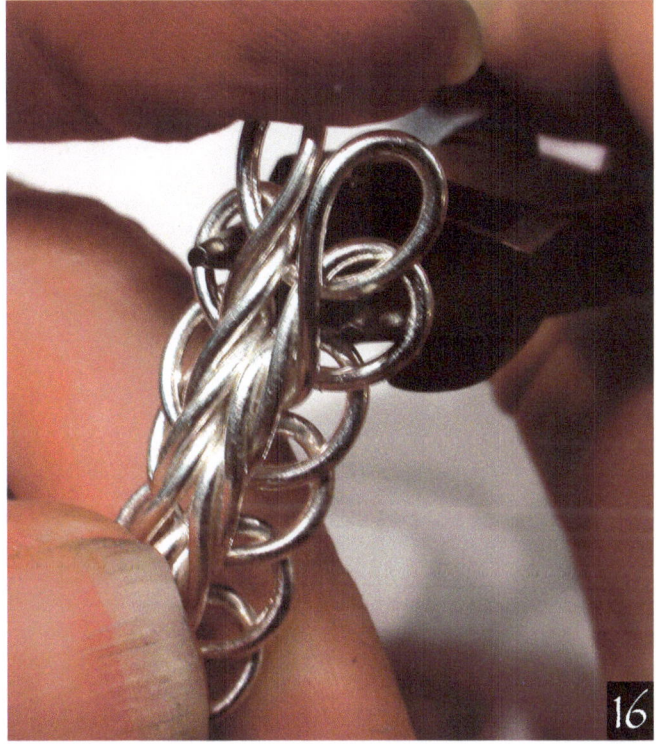

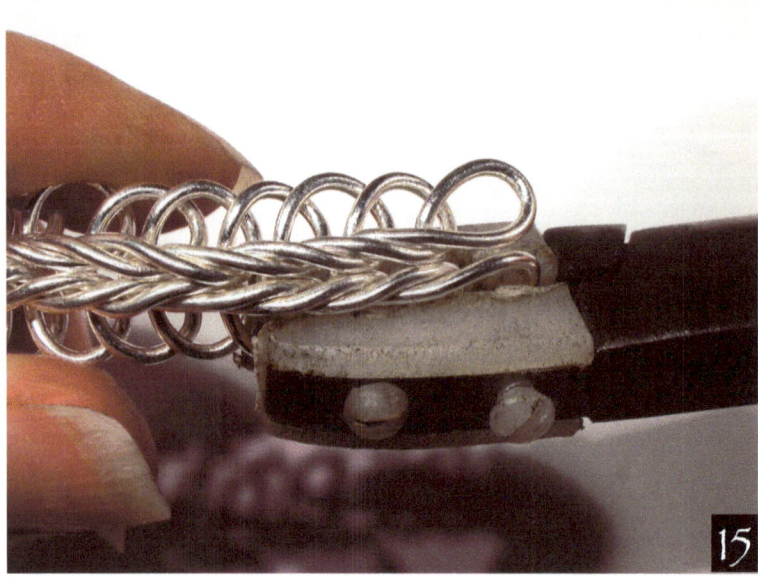

More complex ideas include wire and sphere granulation, kum boo, or Russian filigree.

Anything goes as long as more fragile areas, such as sphere granulation, kum boo, or softer stones are set down in the construction just a bit or aren't too near the edges where they might get dinged or chipped.

15 Sometimes in the process of pinching the braid and opening the side loops, the chain can be accidentally flattened. To regain or create more dimension, use nylon flat pliers to bend the side loops downward so that they lay at an angle to the braid.

"Y" Clasp

The decorative top of this clasp is optional. You can follow the direction to make a simple hook or get creative, and make your chain truly one-of-a-kind.

Ideas for for a decorative top include a small roller printed or stamped sheet of 18 or 20 gauge sterling or a large cabochon set in a bezel cup that is backed with a sheet of metal onto which you can solder the hook.

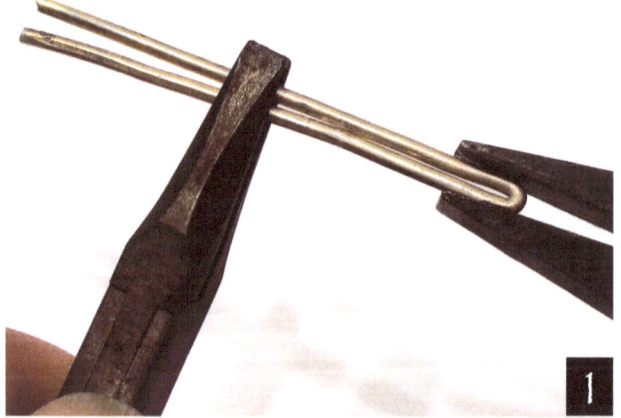

1 Bend a 4" piece of 18 gauge sterling round wire in half. Holding with two pairs of pliers helps to crimp the bend without letting the wire flip.

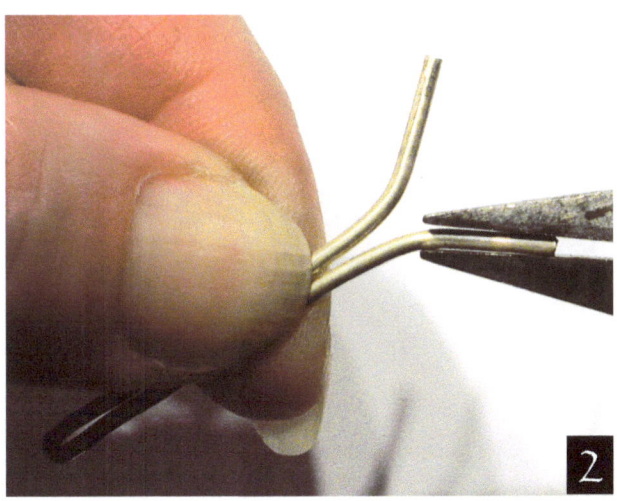

2 Flare out the last 1/2" of the ends into a "Y" shape.

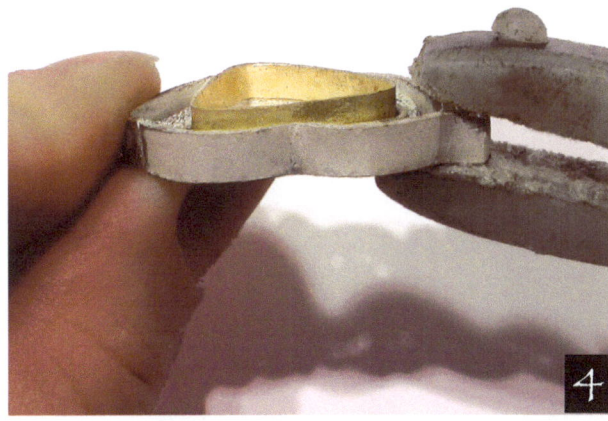

4 The clasp will look and function better if it is slightly curved. If you have a stone setting on your clasp top, bend only the portion that extends beyond it, so that the setting will not warp.

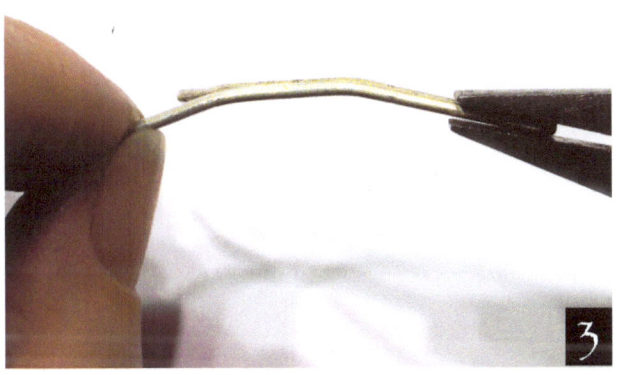

3 If soldering the hook to a decorative element, bend the wire down slightly at the beginning of the "Y" and also half way from there to the end. If you are making a plain hook, go to step 5.

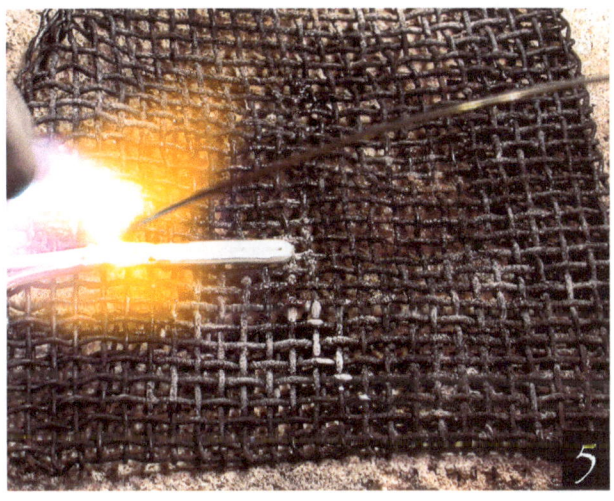

5 Flow easy solder where the wires touch. If soldering to a decorative top, leave a lump of solder on top of the center section of the hook. If not, proceed to step 7.

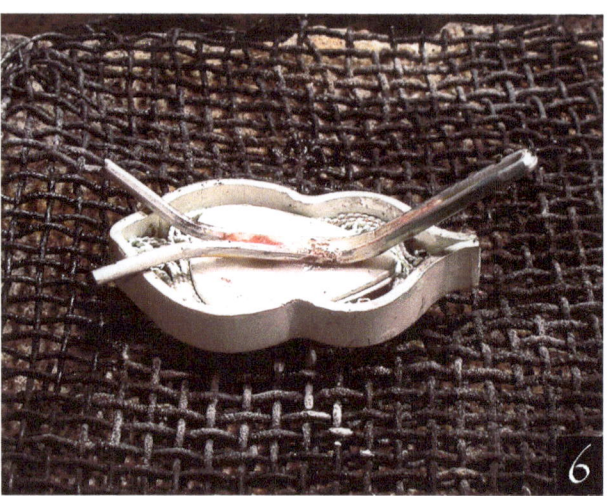

6 Lay the clasp on the back of the fluxed decorative top. Heat all over so that the lump of solder on the underside of the hook re-flows, joining the pieces together.

Soldering Tip!

Remember that silver is a good conductor of heat, so when soldering, the heat must be evenly distributed throughout a piece to make the solder flow. Aiming the torch at the hook portion alone will likely melt it long before the solder re-flows. Instead, move your torch quickly around the decorative top and let the hook become hot by conduction.

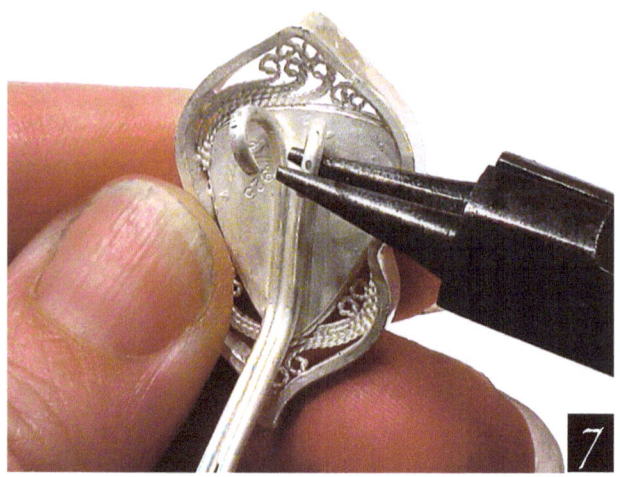

7 With round pliers, bend each part of the "Y" into a loop, leaving them slightly open. With flat pliers, adjust their angle so that they are almost parallel to each other.

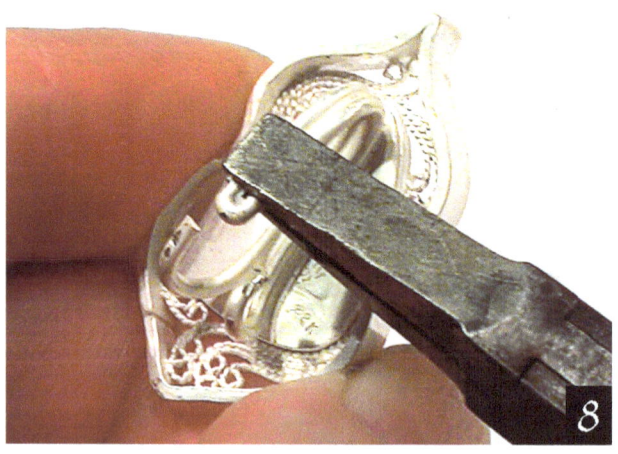

6 Bend the end of the hook over with flat pliers.

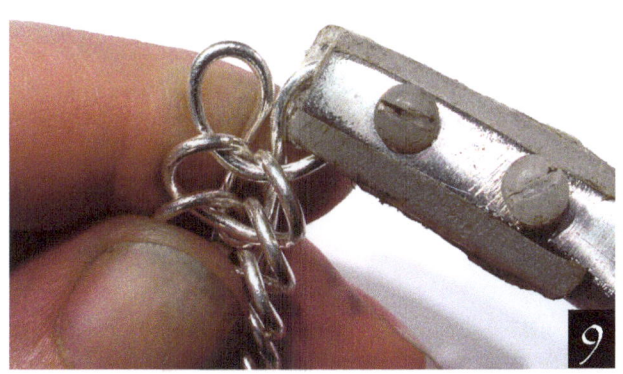

9 Flare out the side loops of the first link in your chain.

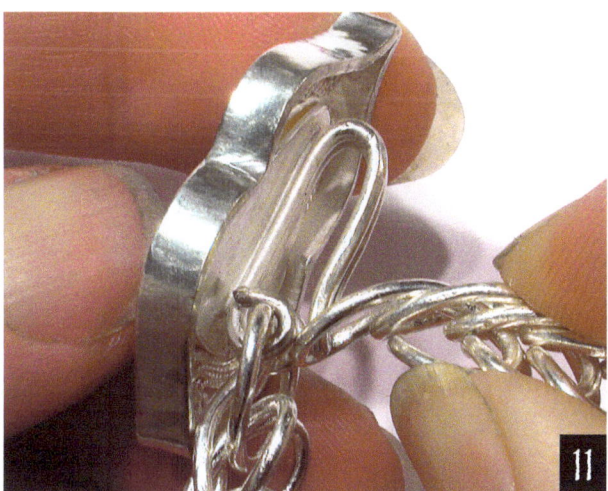

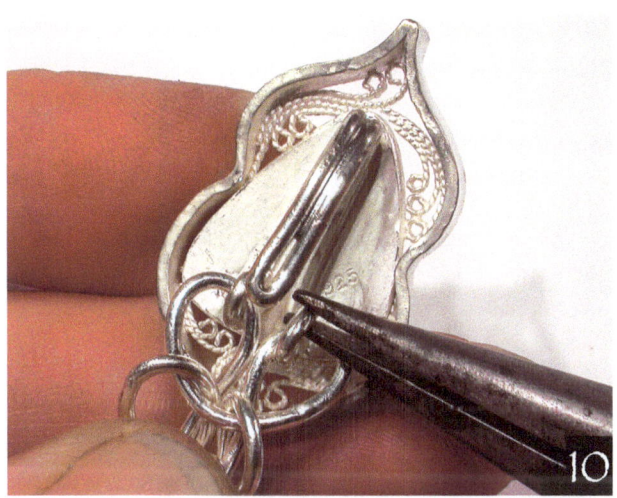

10 Attach the end of the chain to the loops of the hook, and close the loops so that they touch either the hook or the back of the decorative top with no gaps.

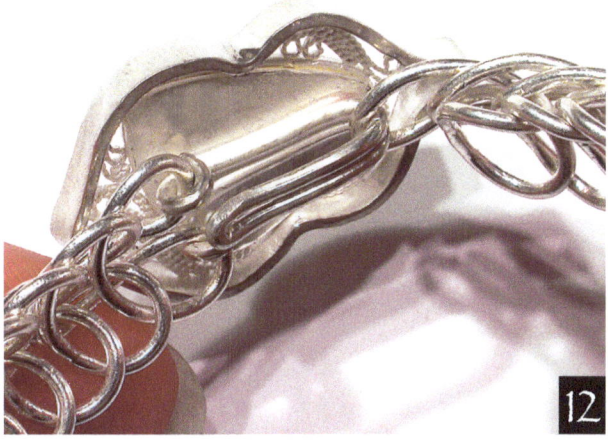

11-12 Use a scriber to round and open up the long loop of the final link. This becomes the jump ring. Compress the bar so that the link cannot come loose.

Adjust the bend of the hook so that it flares out slightly at the tip, making it easier to hook the chain. The hook portion should be bent over enough to create a little tension where it meets the hook's loops, which will keep the chain from unhooking too easily.

Vertebrate Variations

This chain can be made in any gauge from 14 through 22. Chains too long to fit someone are easily adjustable.   Just remove the last link or two, and repeat step 11 to make a jump ring out of the long loop of the last link.   Using 14 gauge with the same size mandrel of 19 mm, makes a large tightly woven chain that is great for men's bracelets. The links can become very work hardened, so anneal them after forming to make opening them up with the scriber much less laborious. Pile up the links on a charcoal block and mark a few of them with a black permanent marker. Heat the whole pile. When the marker ink disappears, the links are annealed.

Another of my favorite variations is 20 gauge wire with a 13mm mandrel. Vertebrate chains bend laterally and can be used for necklaces as well. *Undulation* (right) is an example of a smaller Vertebrate that can be worn as a choker or a necklace. I made the chain adjustable by attaching 6 links formed and woven in the 1-Direction Single-Weave pattern to the last Vertebrate link.

Experiment with different sizes of links.   If I had worried about doing something incorrectly, I would never have come up with the pattern in the first place! There is no "wrong" way only endless variations.

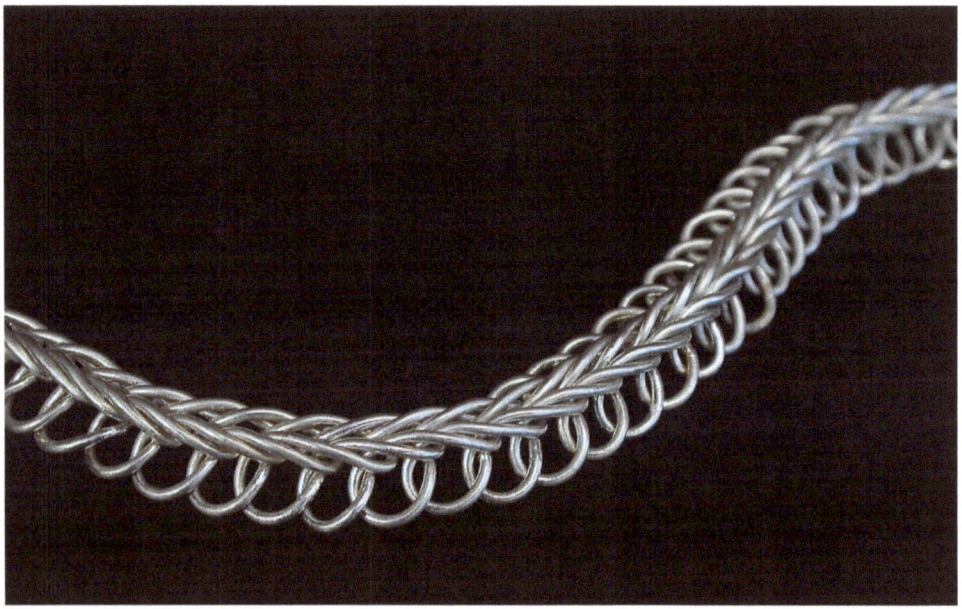

Detail view of a Vertebrate chain made from 20 gauge fine silver round wire and a 13mm mandrel

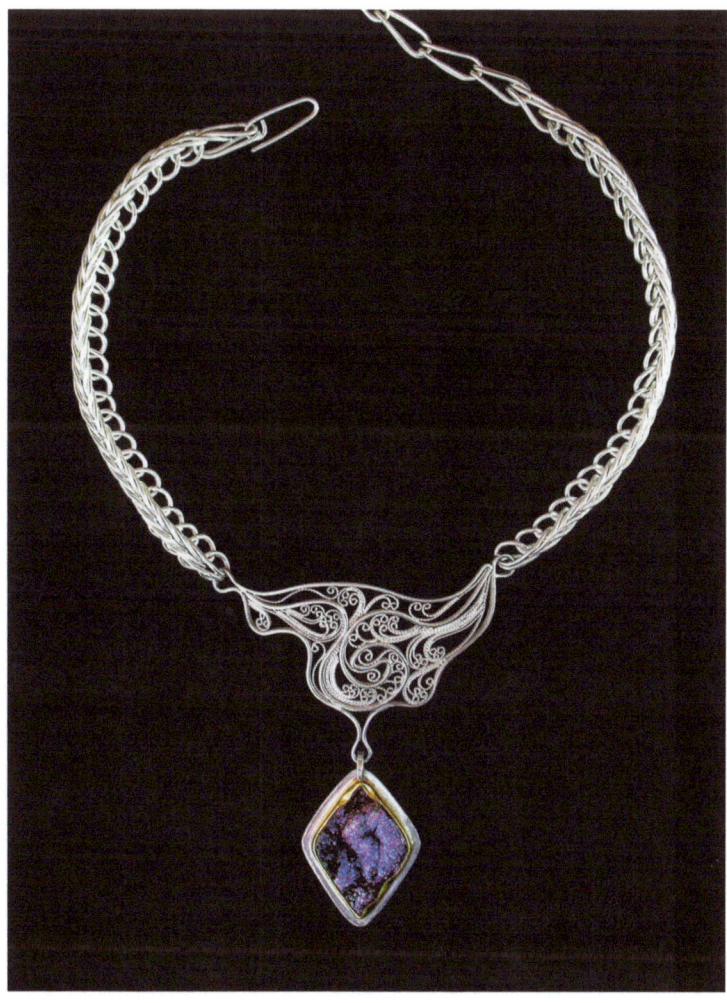

Undulation

Russian filigree and Vertebrate chain necklace/choker; 22k gold,
sterling silver, fine silver, titanium bonded chalcedony drusy; center
piece: 3" long x 3-1/2" wide, chain adjustable to 18" long; 2004

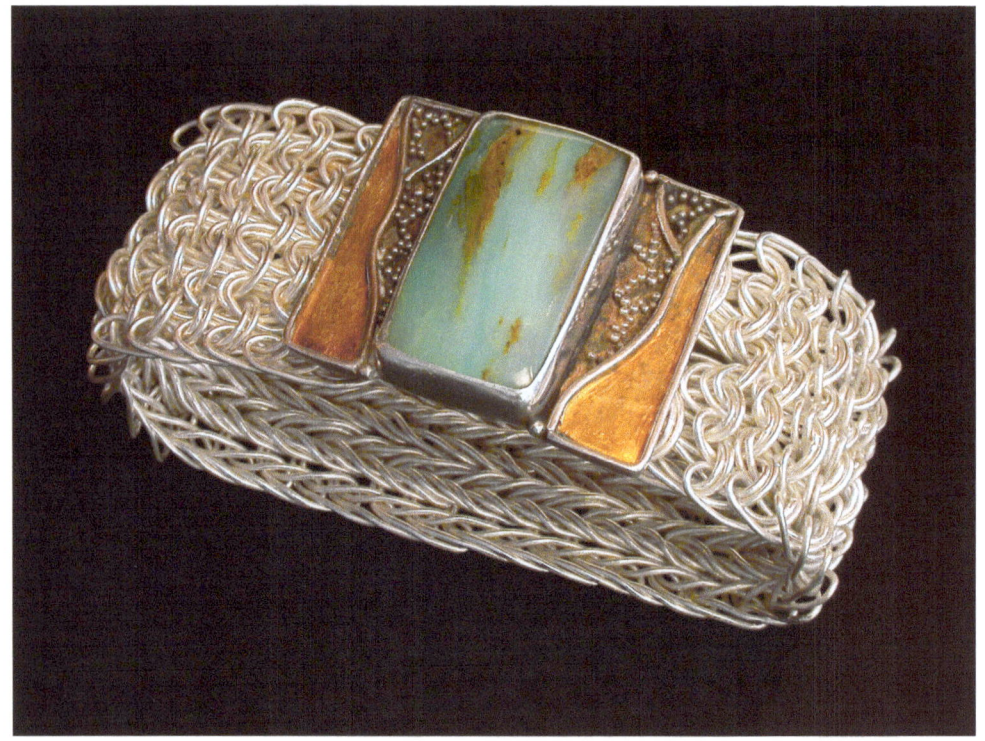

Rivers of Gold VII

Granulation, kum boo, and Side Weave Mesh bracelet; sterling silver, fins silver, 24k gold, Peruvian opal; 7" long x 1-1/2" wide; 2008

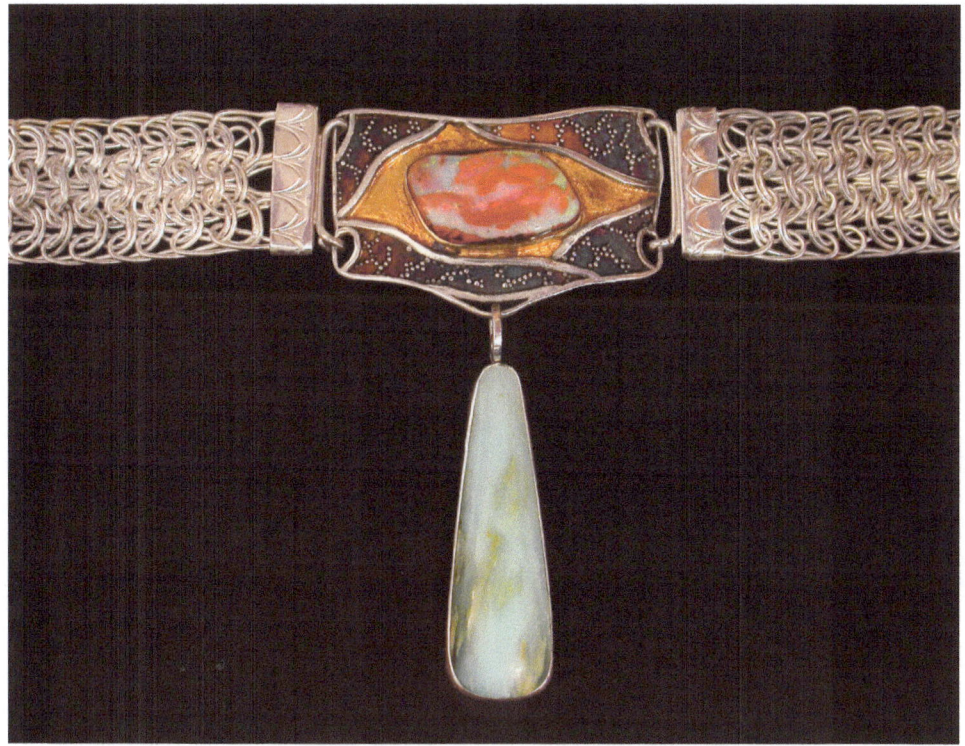

Rivers of Gold VI

Granulation, kum boo, and Side Weave Mesh choker; sterling silver, fins silver, 22k, 24k
gold, Peruvian opal, Koroit opal; 4" long, choker adjustable to 15" long; 2007

Side Weave Mesh

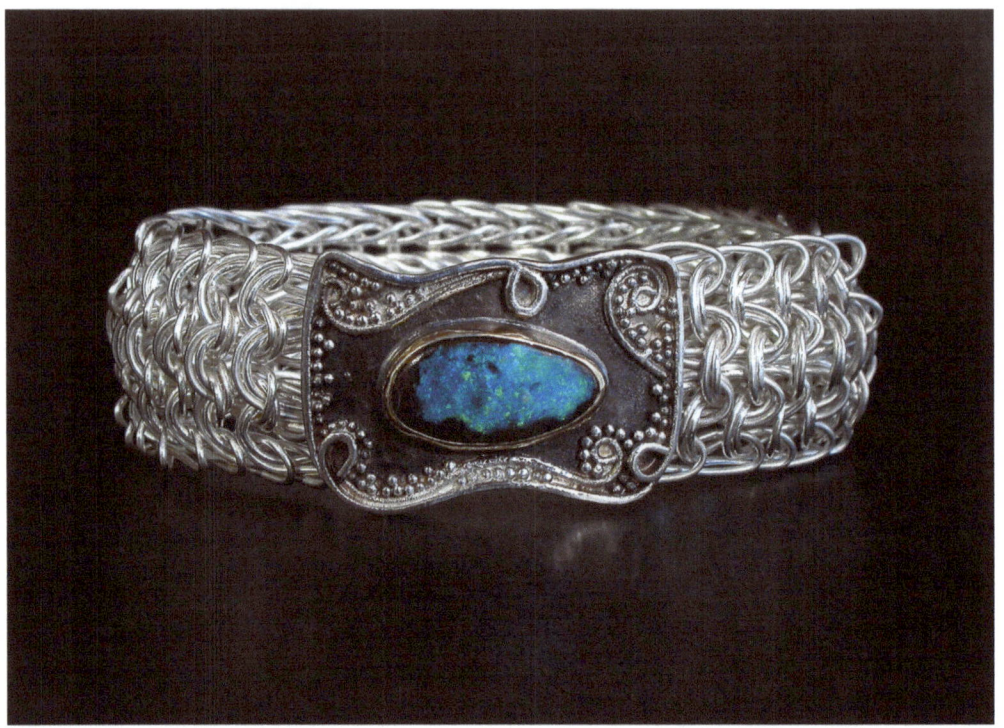

Sea of Blue

Granulation and Side Weave Mesh bracelet; sterling silver, fine silver, 22k gold, Koroit opal; 7"
long x 7/8" wide; 2008

Metal & Mandrel

20 gauge fine silver round wire, 1.75
 ounces for a 7" bracelet
19mm mandrel
12" 18 gauge round or square sterling
 silver wire
metal and stone (optional) for
 decorative top of clasp

This chain is still my favorite of the ones I
invented. What gives it a chain maille
appearance is that it is a double weave like
the vertebrate and many of the ancient
Mediterranean patterns. It is inspired by
the ancient side weave chain. My goal was
to create a wider mesh version with a
repeating pattern based on the flat braid
indicative of one side. Ironically, it was

the herringbone design of the back of the Side Weave Mesh that became my obsession.

I was disappointed at first to find that it didn't work the way I'd anticipated, that the herringbone did not turn out particularly refined. I was about to give up when I looked at what I'd thought of as the chain's back. This former back side that I now consider the front was far more interesting than I'd expected.

Once in a while I teach this chain to someone, who weaves it so meticulously that the back is as beautiful as the front such as Clarissa Urutia's choker (page 93). One of the most satisfying things about teaching is not only when a student's creativity is unleashed in a whole different direction, but also when her/his technique exceeds mine.

means the links can melt easily. Do not despair, however, as the melted links can be used for a bonus chain described later.

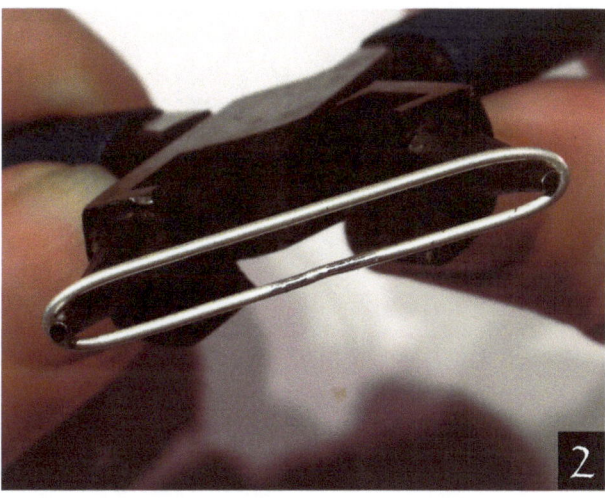

2 Stretch the links open on the tips of round nose pliers that open wide. The seam should be in the middle, where it will receive the least compression.

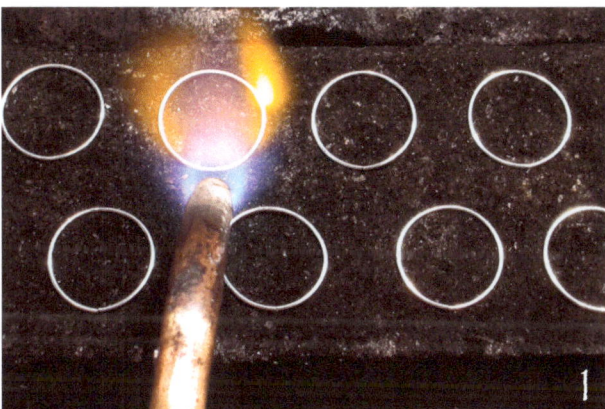

1 Fuse 20 gauge links in the same manner as the other chains (page 12). The challenge here is that the links are large, but the wire gauge is much smaller, which

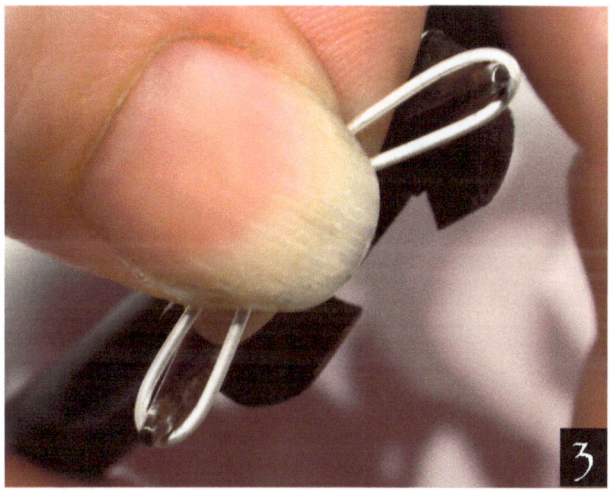

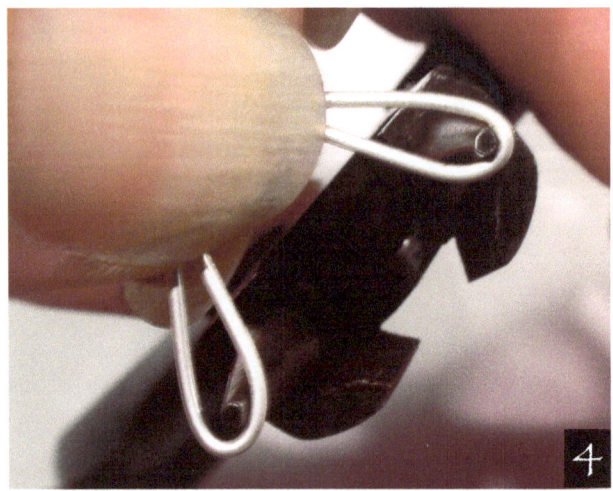

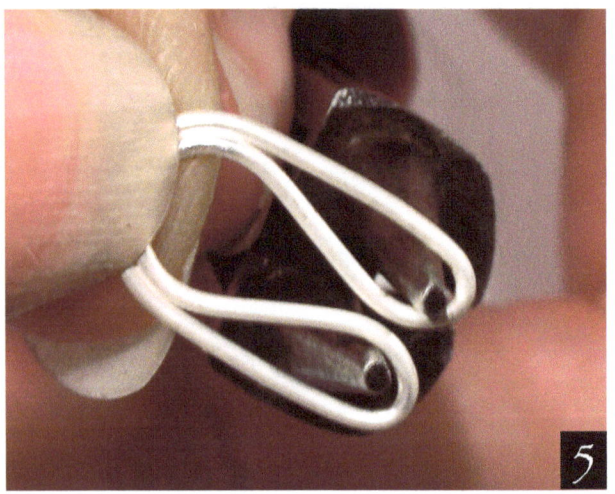

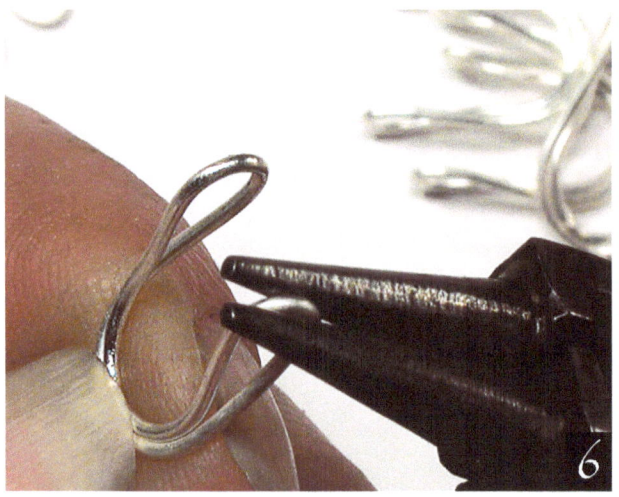

6 Turn the loops outward 90 degrees. Turning the loops makes it possible to weave them into the chain much the same way that pinching the links does for many of the ancient Mediterranean chain patterns. For the last three links, stop at step 5, prior to turning out the loops.

3-5 Grasp the link in the middle with your thumb and index finger. Pull the middle back, letting the pliers close as you pull. Keep pulling until the ends of the loop

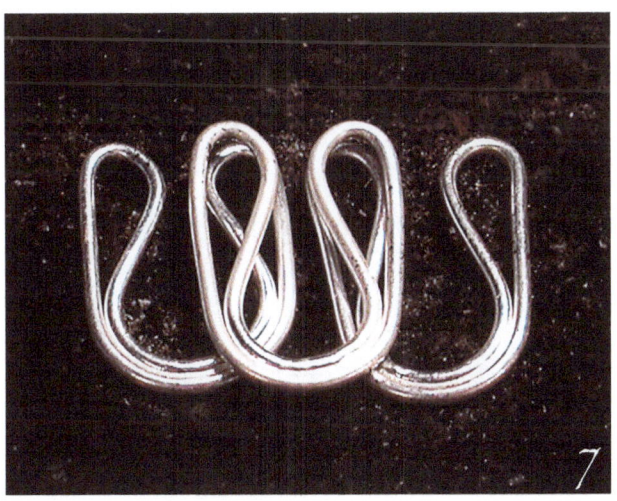

7 Place two of the flat links side by side on a charcoal or other soldering block. Lay the third flat link on top of the two links so that the loops line up. Solder the links with easy solder where they touch at the top. Also allow the solder to flow along the middle of each link. This soldered starter link will serve as a jump ring.

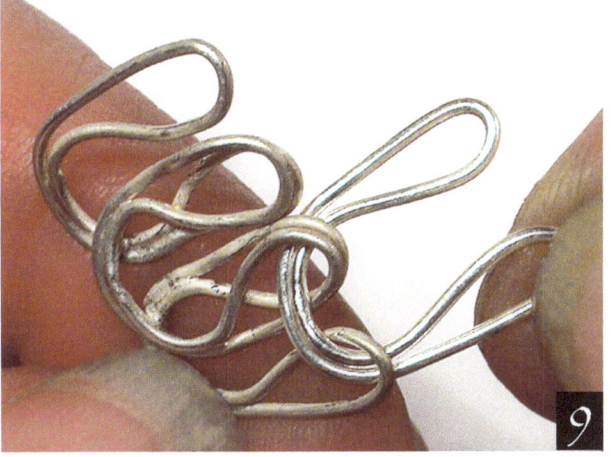

8-9 This chain weaves from the top. Weave a link through the two outside loops on the right of the soldered starter link. Turn the loops back flat. Repeat this step on the left set of loops

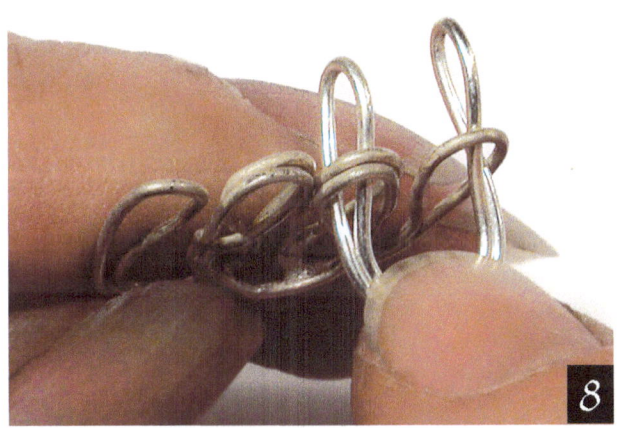

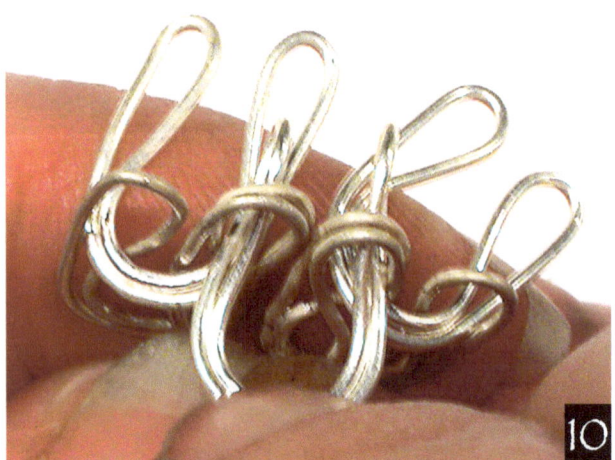

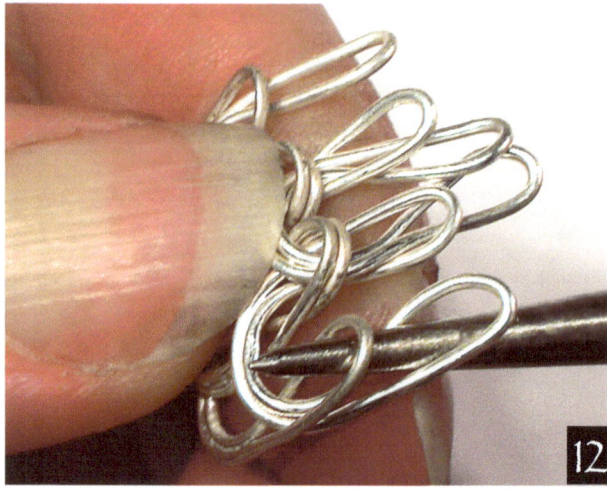

12   From the back, insert the scriber through both of the outside right loops to open them up.

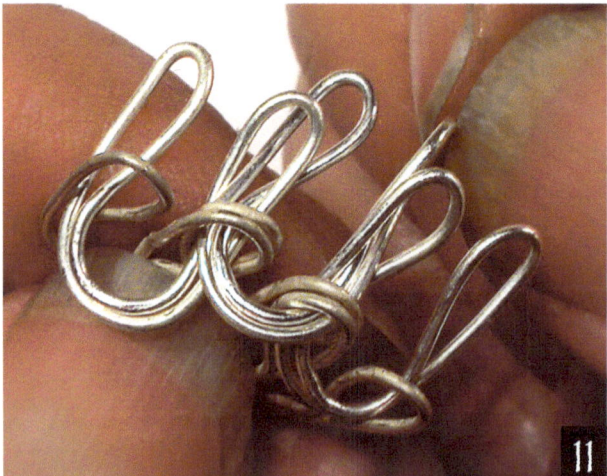

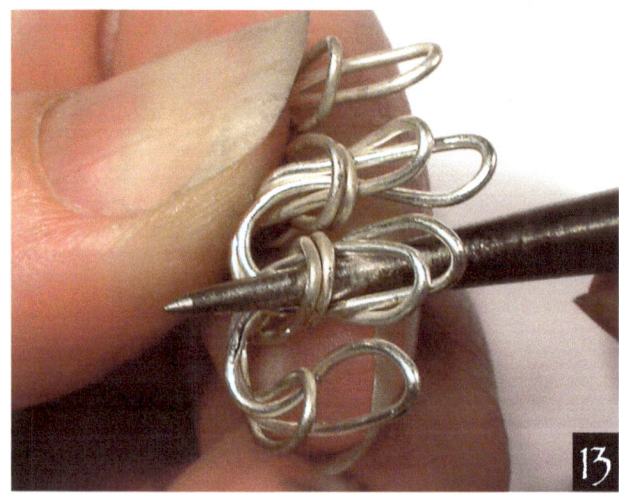

10-11   Hold the soldered starter link, letting the two new links flop forward. Insert another link in the two doubled inside loops.   As you push this link through, also insert it through the inside loops of the two outside links you just wove. Turn the loops flat.

13   Insert the scriber through all four of the loops on the inside right.

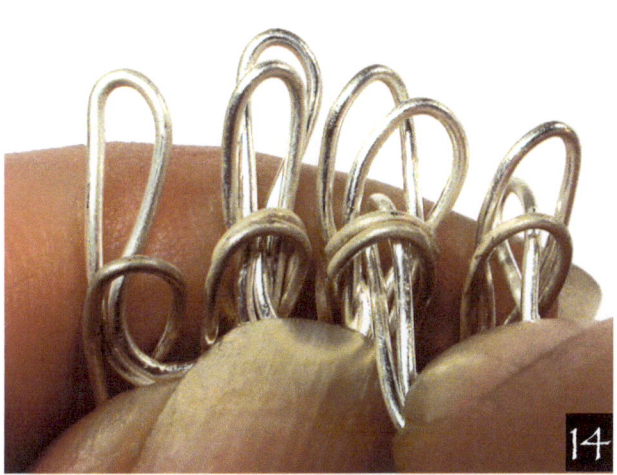

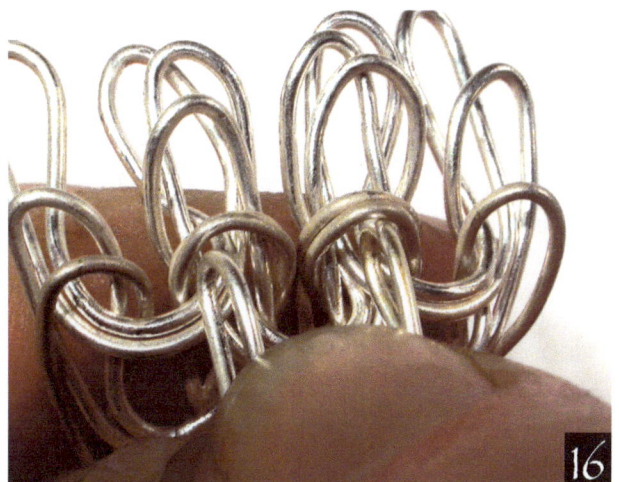

14 Insert a link through two loops on the outside right and *four* loops on the inside right. Turn the loops flat. Repeat steps 12-14 for the two sets of loops on the left.

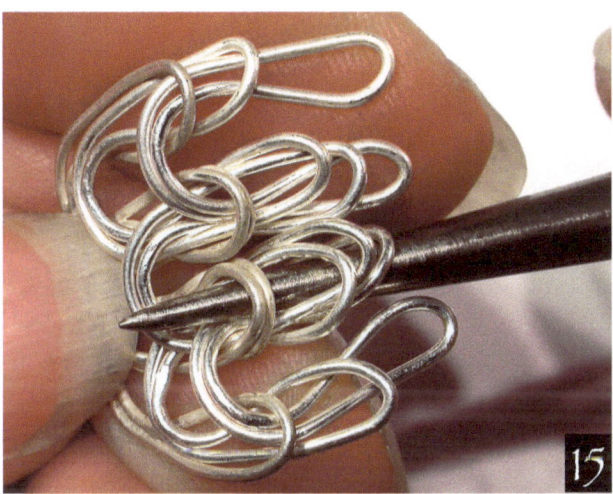

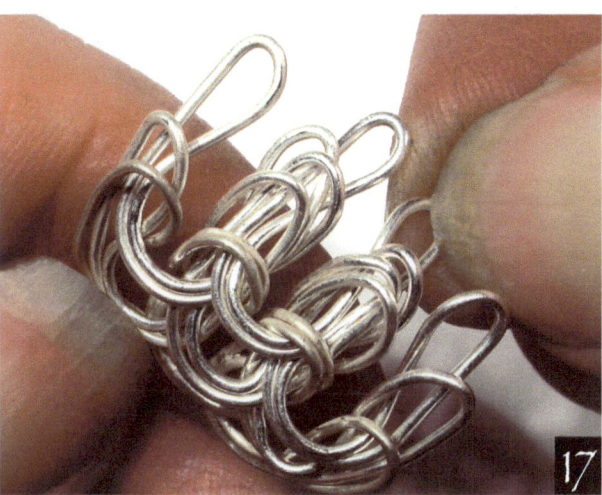

15 From the back insert the scriber and open up all four loops of the inside right and inside left sets of loops.

16-17 Insert a link through all four of the inside right and left sets of loops and on top of the links you just wove on the outside right and left. Once the new link has gone through those four loops on each side, push it on through the inside loops of the new links on the right and left.

Confused?

Breathe. From the third row on, each link is woven through the two previous links each time. The middle link creates lots of extra loops, which can be difficult to manage. The outer links are woven through two and four loops. The middle links are woven through a total of five loops, including the right and left links on the same row.

The pattern becomes Right 2 & 4; Left 2 & 4; Middle 5 & 5. The first 4 rows are difficult to weave because there is little chain to hold onto, and the links wiggle around. If you can keep going past the fourth row, the chain will become much easier to weave.

Repeat this step on the outside left loops.

Repeat steps 15-17 for the middle link. Continue weaving in this manner until the chain is just long enough to wrap around your wrist. The clasp will provide enough slack to make the chain fit comfortably.

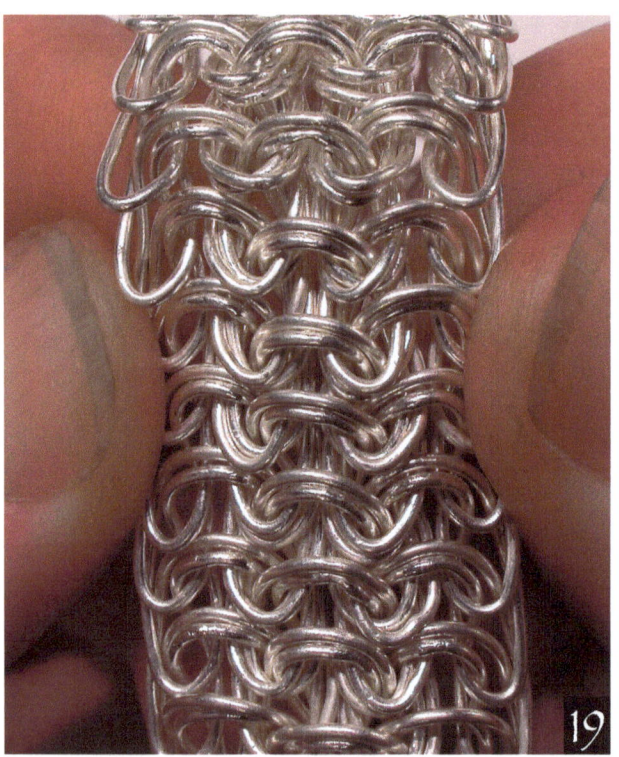

19 The chain has a tendency to flare out at the edges during the weaving process. To correct this, curve the outer loops slightly downward with your fingers. The chain may be polished with a SparkleSparkle Ultracloth or with blue rouge on a mini muslin buff on the flex shaft.

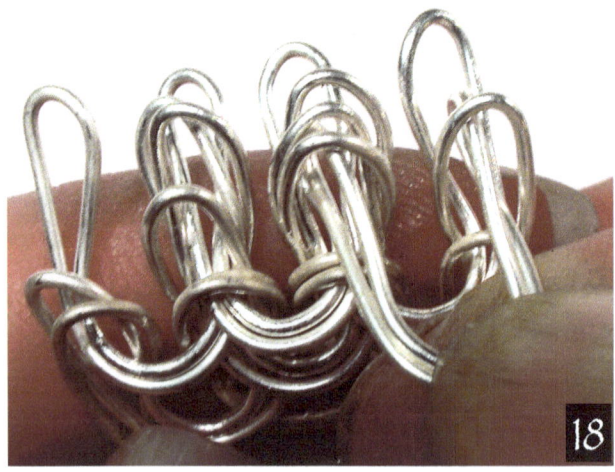

18 After opening the outside right loops with a scriber, insert a link through the two and four loops as described in step 14.

Decorative Clasp

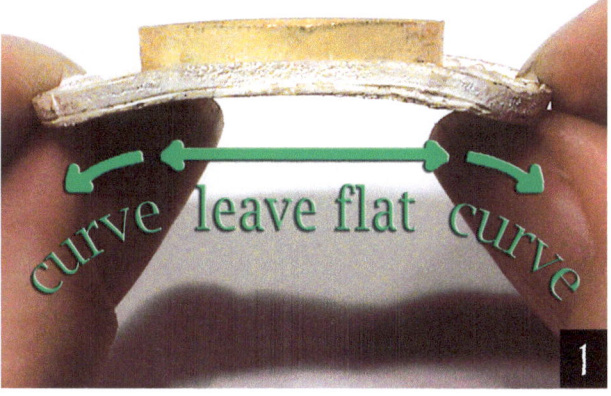

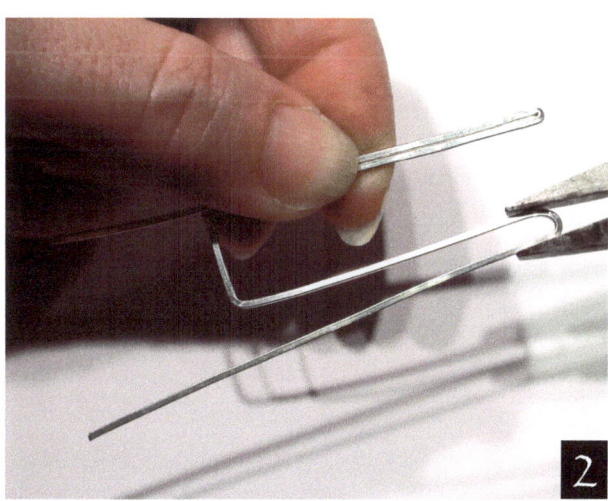

2 Bend 18 gauge square or round sterling wire into a squared "U" shape. The width of the "U" should be the same as the width of your chain. 2" up from the bottom of the "U" bend and crimp the wire back on itself so the sides of the "U" are doubled and the ends of the wire protrude at least 3/4" beyond the bottom of the "U".

1 The double hook for this clasp requires a decorative top to stabilize it and to cover the end of the chain. For decorative ideas see the "Y" clasp in the Vertebrate chapter (page 72). The clasp will look and function better if it is slightly curved. Don't let that keep you from setting a stone on top. Just use nylon pliers to bend the space between the ends of the setting and the edge of the metal.

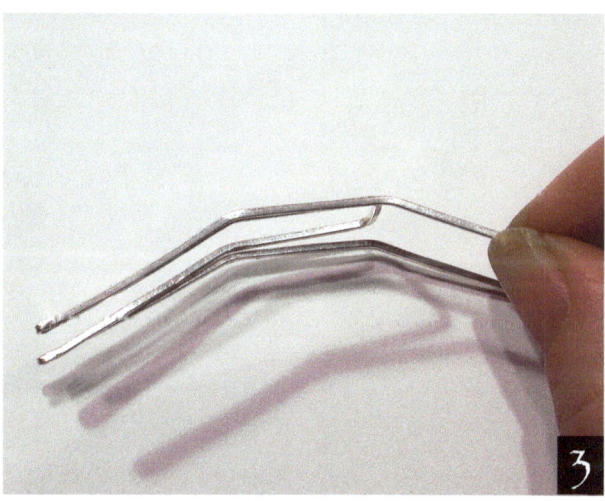

3 With flat pliers, bend the clasp hook downward at a slight angle at the bottom of the "U" and also approximately 3/4" from the bottom of the "U" on the doubled side.

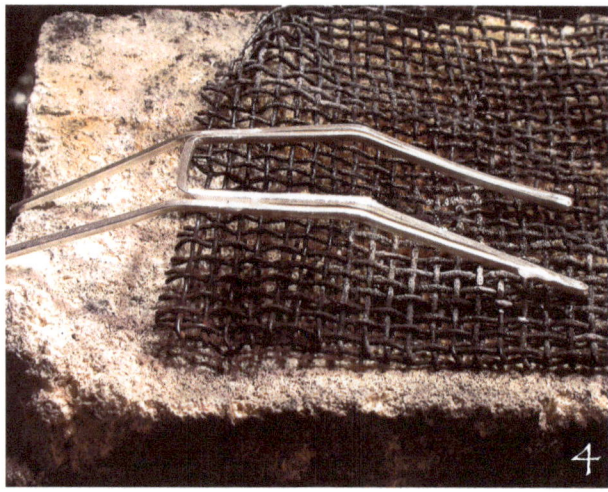

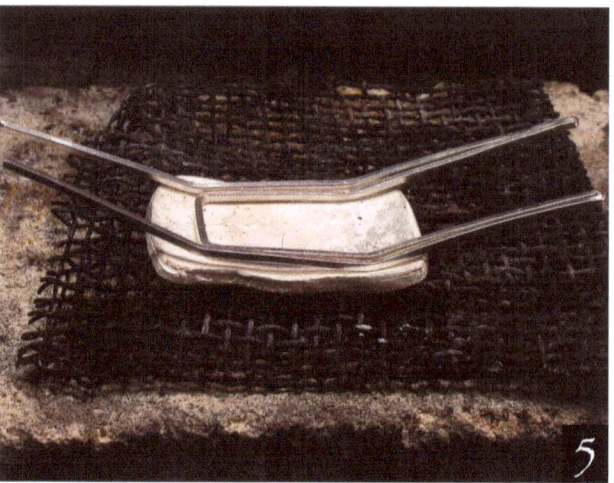

5 Lay the hook on the back of the decorative top. Move the torch quickly around the top, avoiding the ends of the hook wire. The blob of solder on the hook will re-flow, joining the two parts together. For more tips on soldering, see page 72 in the Vertebrate chapter.

4 You will sweat solder the hook onto the decorative top of the clasp. The first step is to flow easy solder on the center section, letting it flow into the space of the doubled wire and blob a tiny bit on the center top.

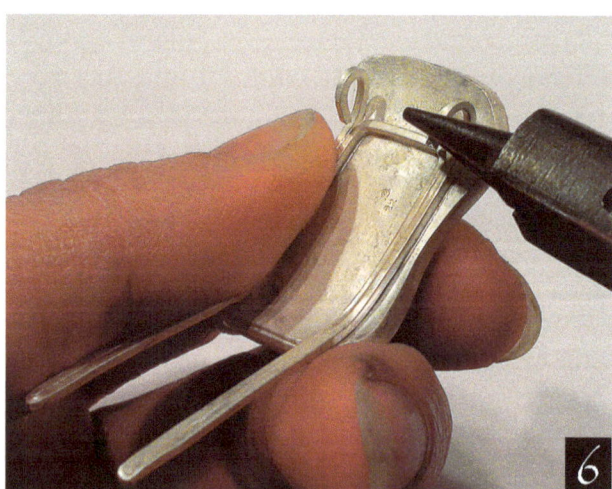

6 Use round pliers to bend over the ends of the wire into loops. These ends may need to be trimmed first.

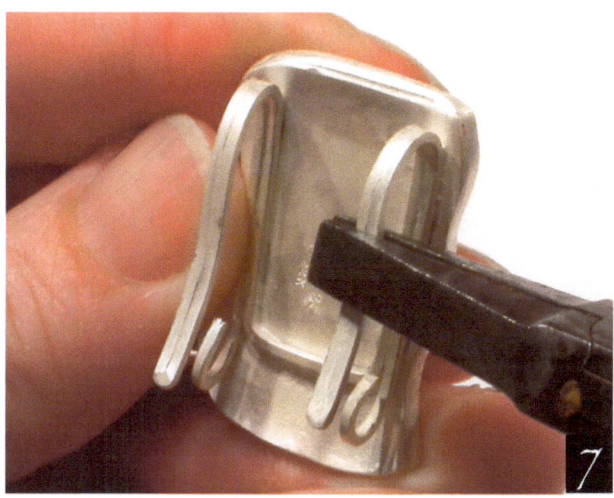

8 To close off the end of the chain, push the last outside right loop in between the two last inside right loops. Open up this three loop set with a scriber. Repeat this step for the loops on the left side.

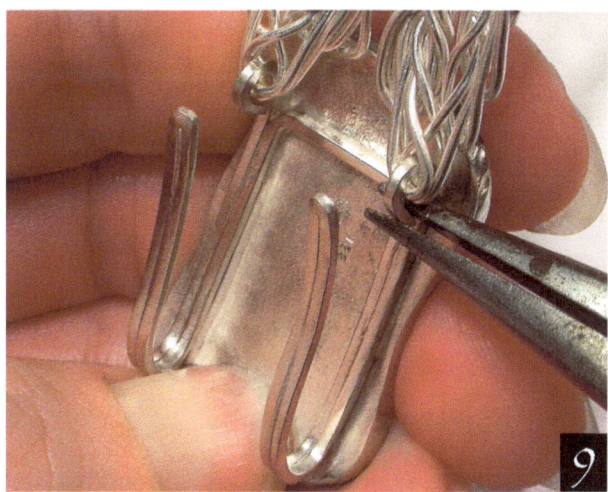

7 Bend over the doubled wires. Gently curve them so that they slope down in the center and flare up slightly at the tips, which makes the bracelet easier to put on.

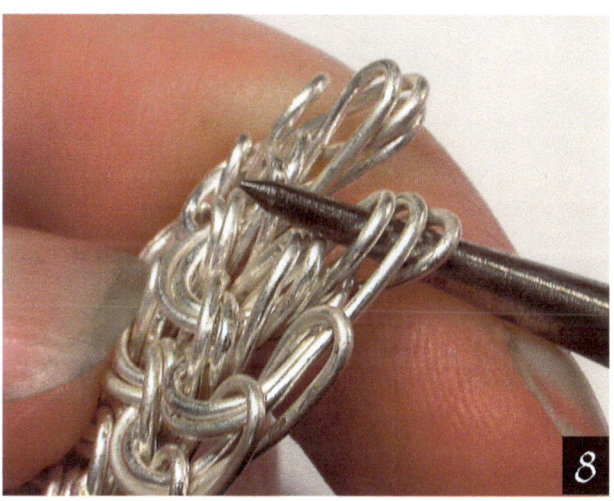

9 Set your stone and clean up and polish the finished clasp. Attach the three loop sets of the chain to the loops of the hook, and close them with chain nose pliers.

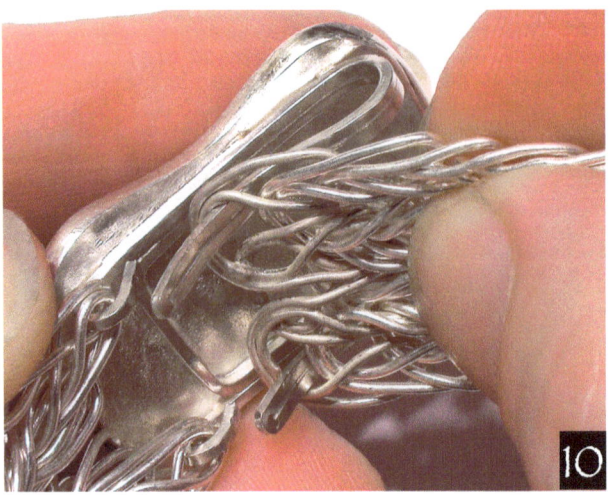

10 Adjust the hooks so that there is a tension spot in the middle as the two outside holes of the soldered starter link slide over the them.

Middle 4 & 4; Left 2 & 4; Middle Right 5 & 5; Middle Left 5& 5. Once you make a three wide, the five wide is rather intuitive. Ok, yes, it takes a lot of links, but it's worth it!

For most of my chokers, two chains are hooked to a center medallion or soldered into flat end caps. The clasp is in the back, and the chain tapers toward the back to make it more comfortable. To taper the chain, repeat step 8 of the clasp until you are left with a one set of double loops, or one row of side weave chain on each chain. On one chain, cross the loops, and attach a basic clasp (page 23). For the other chain weave additional side weave links, or cross the loops of the last one and weave additional 1-Direction Single-Weave chain to make the choker adjustable.

Variations

This project is three links wide. The chain can also be woven five links wide. Any odd number of links will work. For a five link chain, the soldered starter chain is three links side by side with two links soldered on top. The pattern is Right 2 & 4;

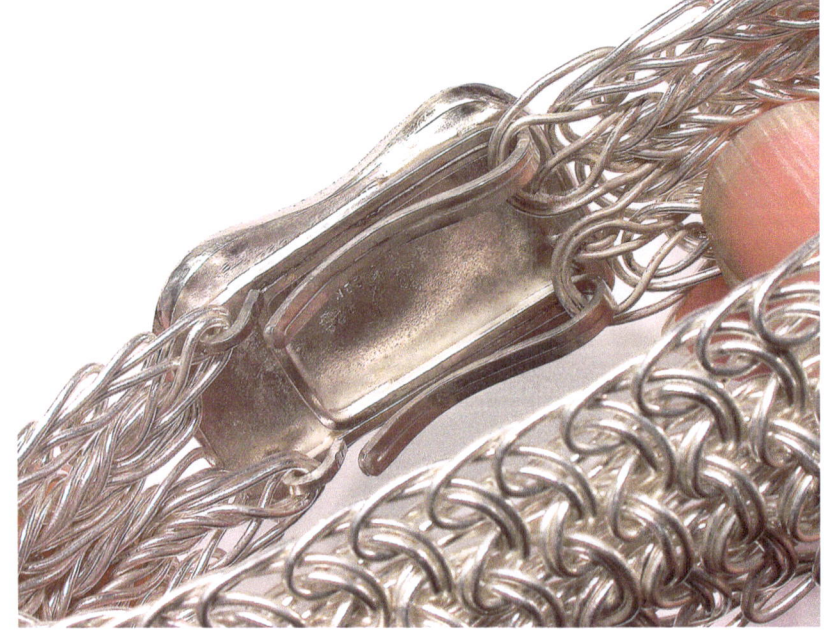

Inside view of the bracelet
Note how the top of the clasp
covers up the less attractive
ends of the chain.

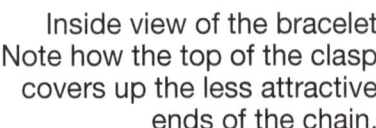

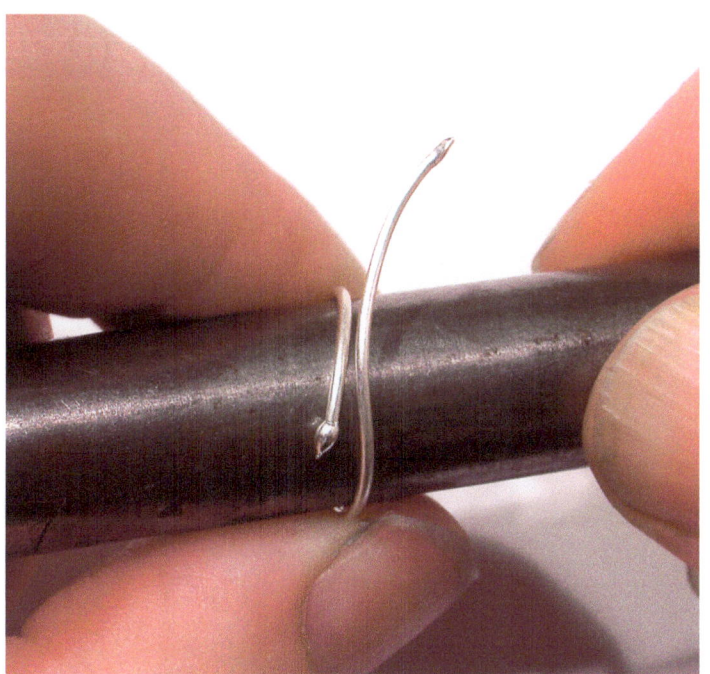

Bonus Chain

Got tons of unusable links leftover? Make a bonus small Vertebrate chain. Wrap each gnarly link around a 13mm mandrel and cut the excess in a place away from the bumps and thin spots. Follow the directions for the Vertebrate chain variation on page 76.

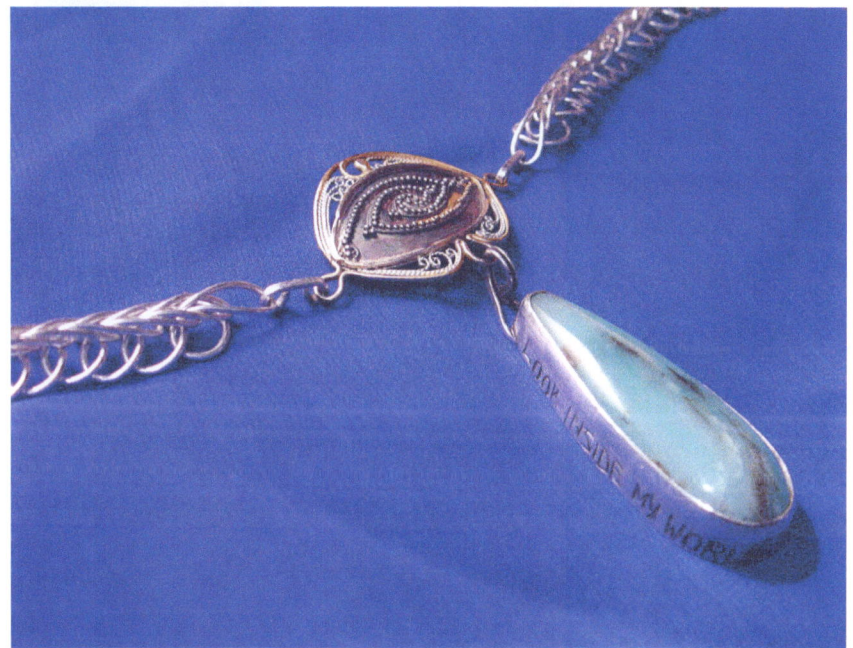

Look Inside My World
Russian filigree, granulation, and Vertebrate choker; 2-3/4" long, chain adjustable to 15" long; 18k gold, sterling silver, fine silver, Peruvian opal; 2001

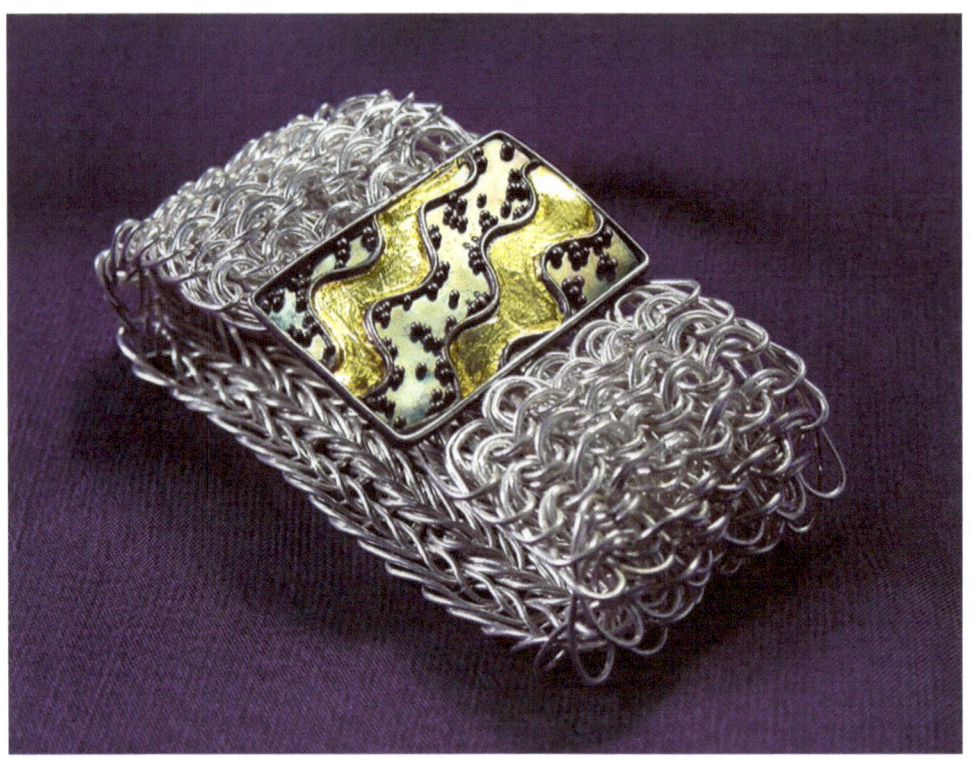

Rivers of Gold

Granulation, kum boo, and Side Weave Mesh bracelet; fine silver, sterling silver, 24k gold;
7" long x 2" wide; 2001

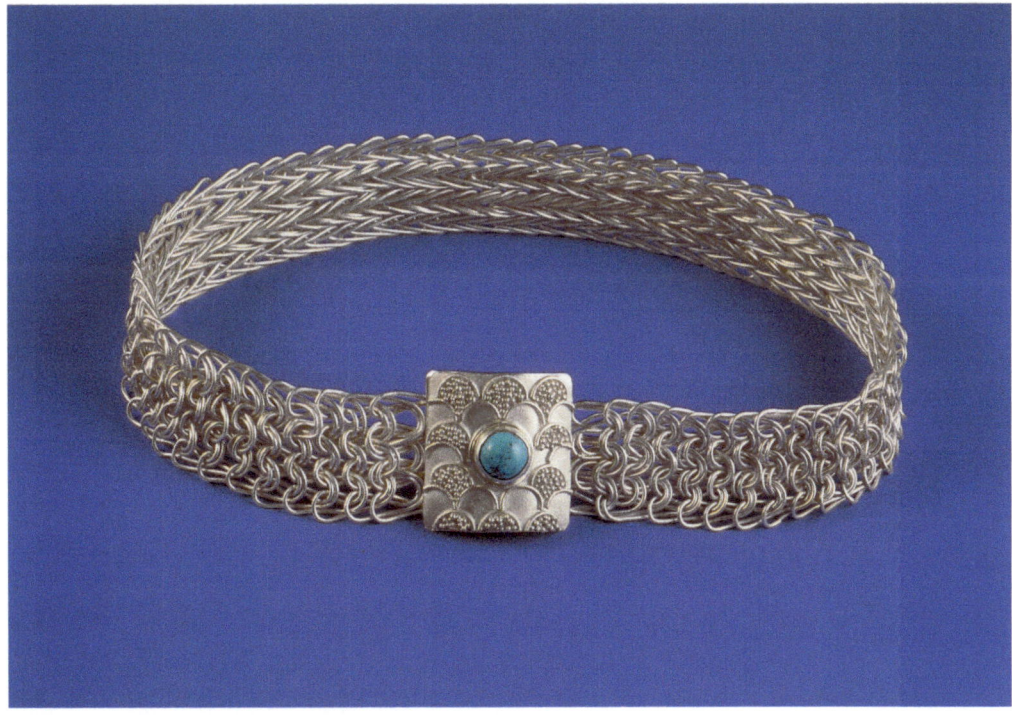

Clarissa Urutia, Untitled
Side Weave Mesh choker with granulation clasp
Sterling silver, fine silver, turquoise; 14" long x 1-14" wide
The clasp detaches from the choker, making the chain reversible.

Crossed Link Chain

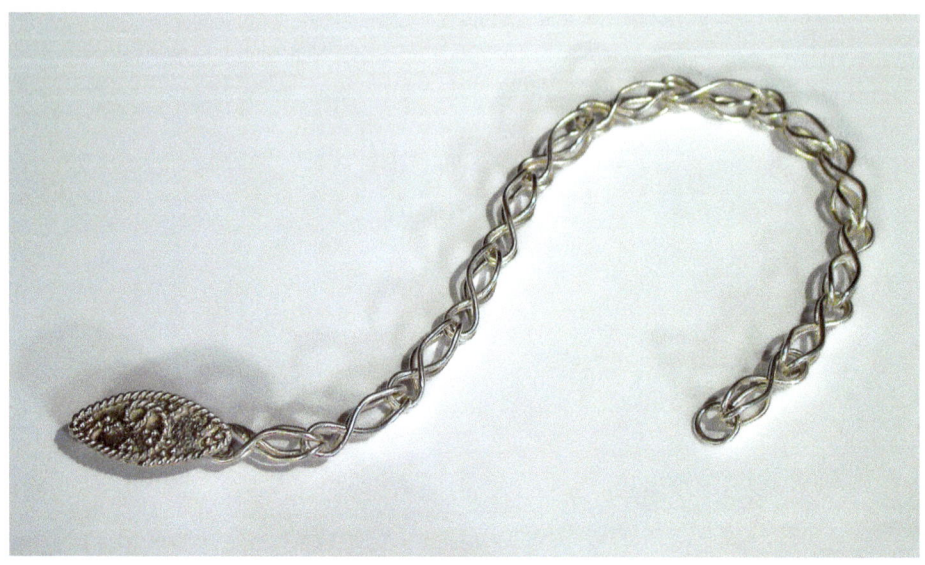

BrainTeaser

Crossed Link chain bracelet with granulation clasp; sterling silver, fine silver ;7" long x
3/8" wide; 2008

Metal & Mandrel

20 gauge fine silver round wire, .75
ounce for a 7" bracelet

19mm mandrel

Solder filled jump ring

1-1/2" 12 gauge sterling half round
wire (or 4" 18 gauge round for
decorative clasp)

Metal and stone for decorative clasp
top (optional)

The Crossed Link chain is my most recent
chain pattern invention. Its inspiration
comes from my love of manipulating links
in ways that resemble knots and will link
together somewhat like the brain teaser
wire puzzles of my childhood. I used to
carry around a small pouch of those kinds
of puzzles. Undoubtedly, I was given them
to occupy my curious brain, but I can
remember bugging everyone around me to
share in the joys of unlocking them.

This chain's beauty lies in its deceptive
simplicity. It weaves just like a 1-Direction
Single-Weave but with a few crisscrosses
going on at the bottom of each link.

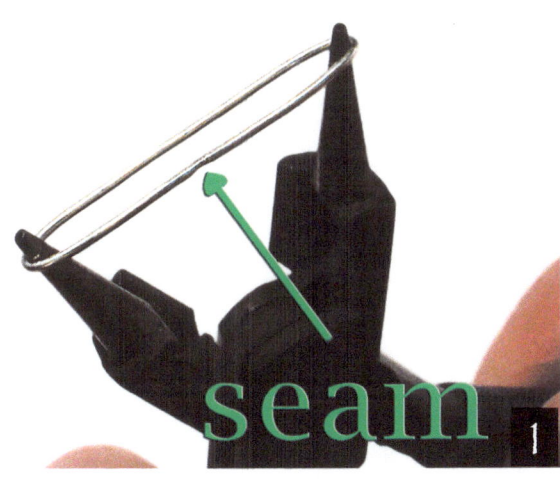

1 Stretch the link on the tips of round nose pliers, making sure that the seam is in the center.

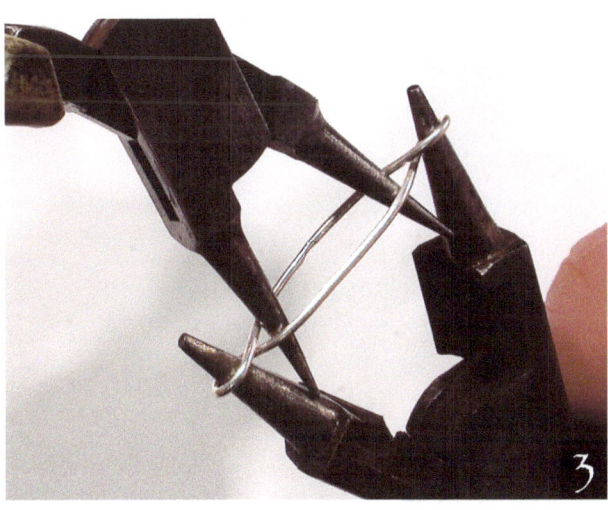

2 Use your thumb and index finger to push the front over the back until they cross near the tips of the pliers.

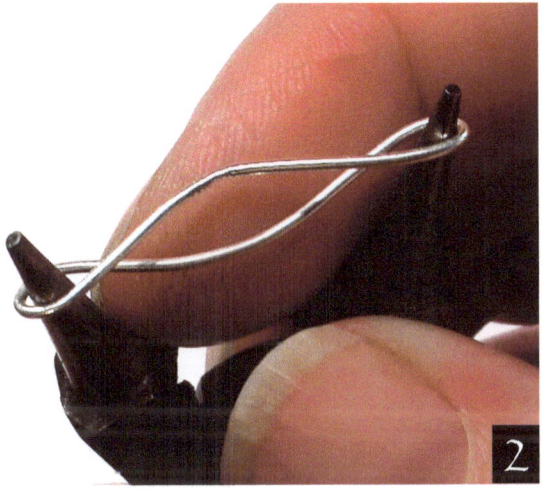

3 With a second pair of round nose pliers, open up the crossed space.

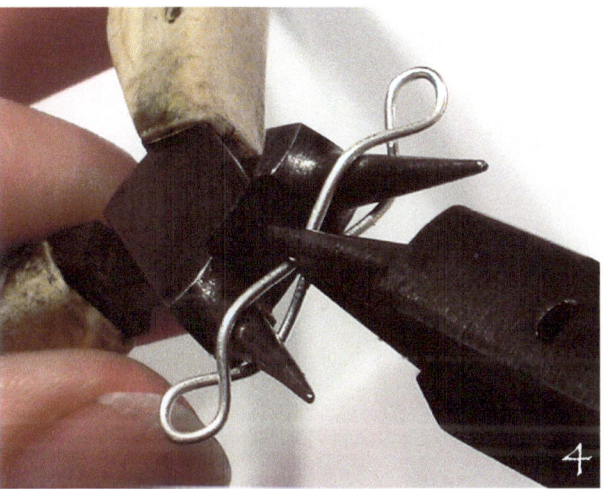

4 Side the lower pliers out of the end loops, and use them to pinch the center of the link.

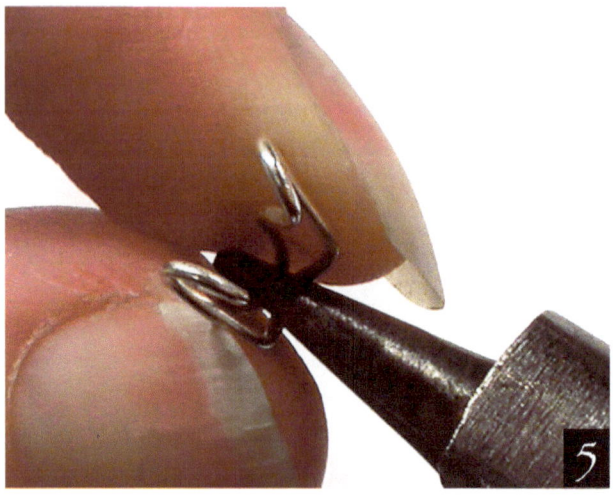

5 Holding the center of the link with round nose pliers, bend the link into a "U" shape.

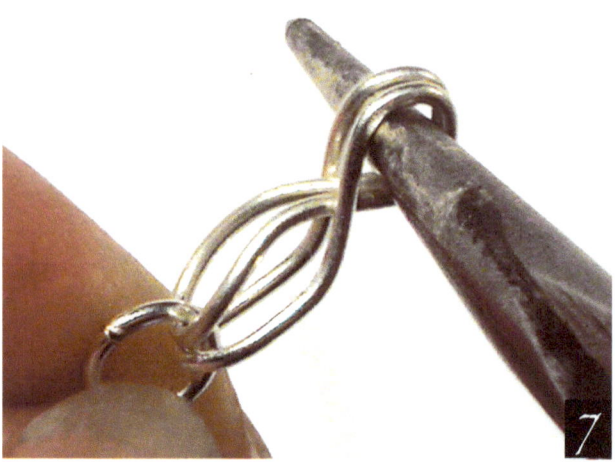

7 Slide a soldered closed, solder filled jump ring over one of the end loops. Pinch the link closed, and open up the end loops with a scriber to make them more rounded.

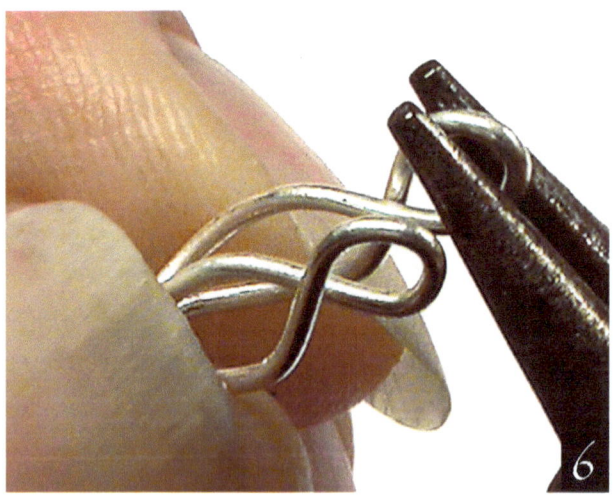

6 Slightly flare out both end loops of the link so that they will touch at the top and at the cross when they are pinched closed.

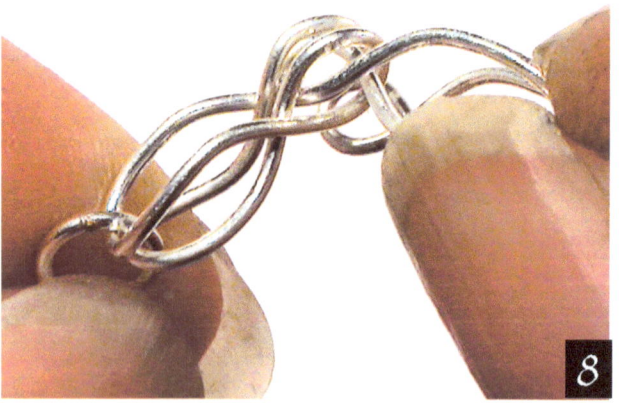

8 Insert one end loop of a new a link through the end loops of the first link and pinch it closed. These links are different

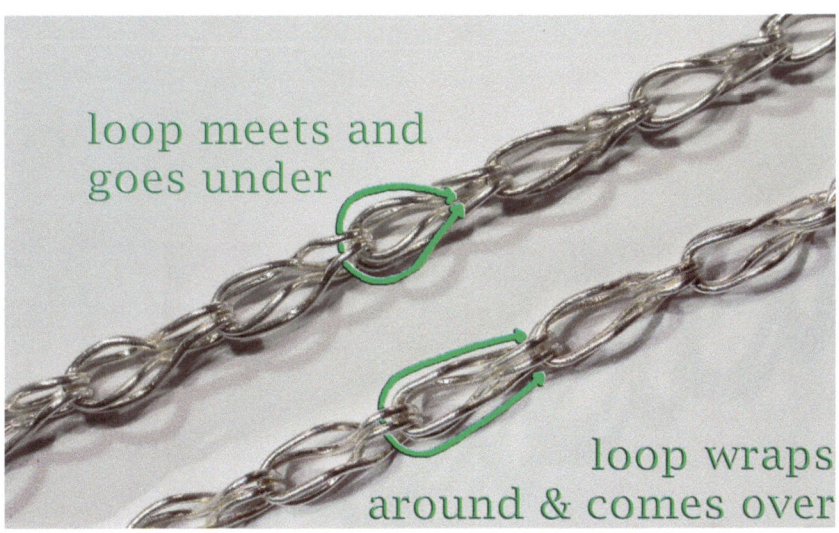

loop meets and
goes under

loop wraps
around & comes over

on each side because of the cross. Be sure that you are weaving them so that each link is crossed the same direction.

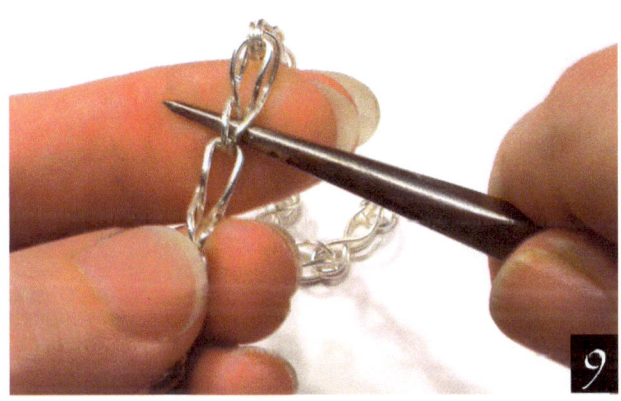

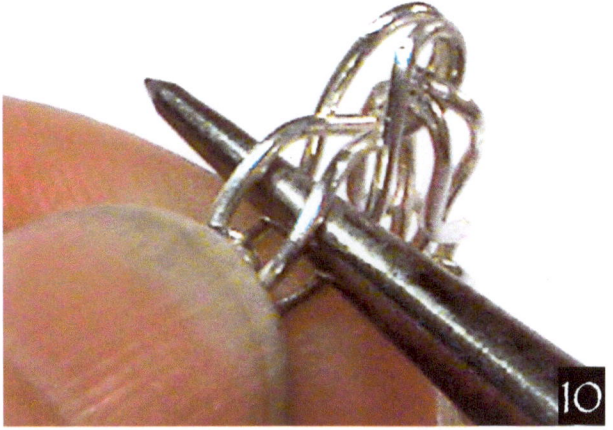

9-10 After the chain is the desired length, insert the scriber up to the same depth in both the end loops and the bottom crossed portions of each link. Repeat this step on the other side of the chain as well to ensure that each link is uniform in shape. Attach a basic (page 23) or decorative clasp to the final end loops.

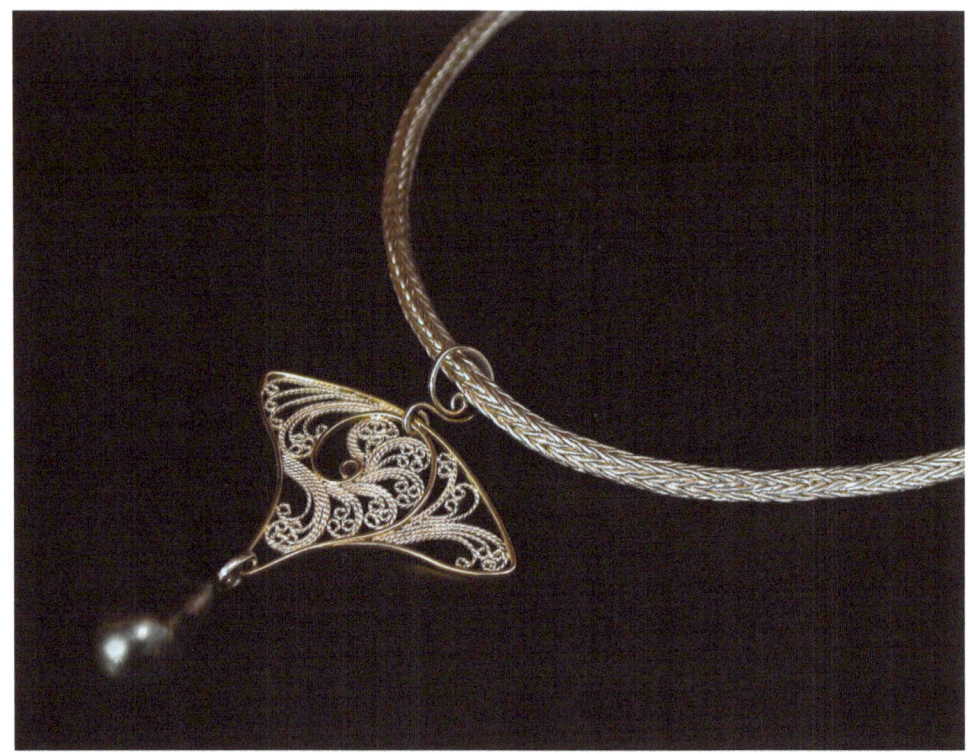

Papyrus Deco III

Russian filigree pendant on a 2-Directional Double-Weave chain; 18k gold, fine silver, sterling silver, Tahitian Pearl; 2" long x 2" wide, 22" chain; 2006

Resources

Tools & Metal

Jewelry Resource Supply
3601 Greenwood Avenue N
Seattle, WA 98103
206-632-7005
www.jewelryresourcesupply.com

Otto Frei
126 2nd Street
Oakland, California 94607
or
760 Market Street, Room # 905
San Francisco, California 94102
800-772-3456
www.ottofrei.com

Rio Grande
800-545-6566
www.riogrande.com

SparkleSparkle Ultracloths™

SparkleSparkle Premium JewelryCare
Nventa Incorporated
6619 East Paradise Lane
Scottsdale, AZ 85254-5603
800-535-4980
CustomerCare@Nventa.com
www.sparklesparkle.com

Metal

David H. Fell & Company, Inc.
6009 Bandini Blvd.
City of Commerce, CA 90040
or
550 S Hill St # 560
Los Angeles, CA 90013
800-822-1996
contact@dhfco.com
www.dhfco.com

Reactive Metals
(Straight Grain Mokume Gane)
PO Box 890
Clarkdale, AZ 86324
800-876-3434
www.reactivemetals.com

Stones

Bill Gangi (Drusies and cabochons)
Box 225
Franklin Square, NY 11010
520-245-4318
gangi@flash.net
www.gangigems.com

Eugene McDevitt (Koroit Opals and other
cabochons)
P.O. Box 55
Safety Harbor, FL 34695
727.742.5471
gene@koroit.com
www.koroit.com

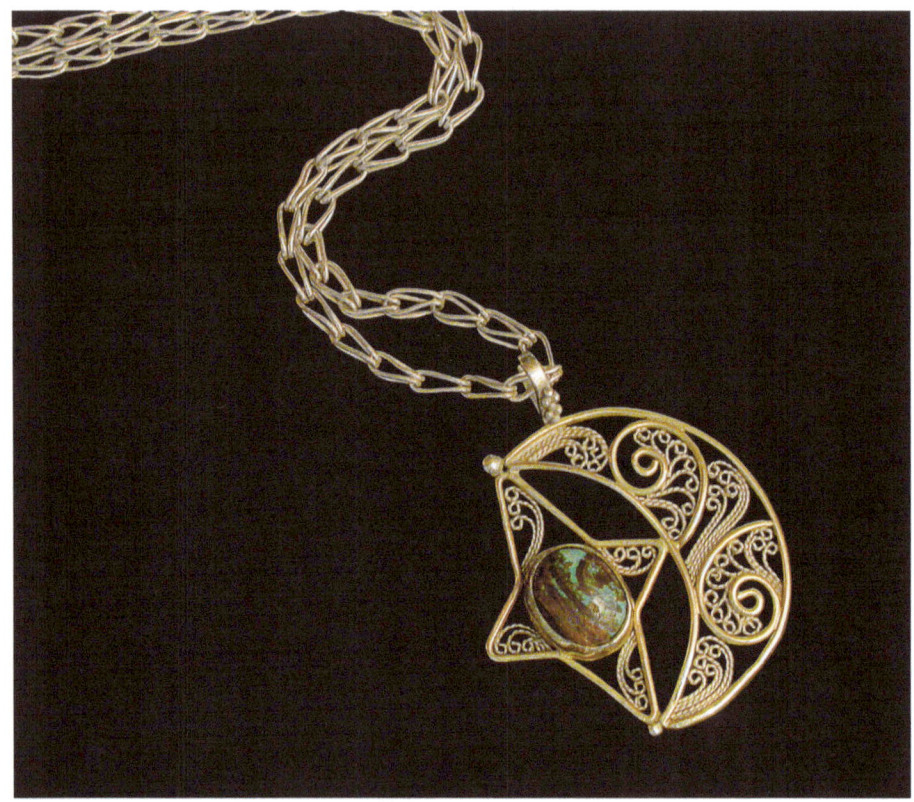

Crescents & Starlight VI

Russian filigree pendant on a 1-Direction Single-Weave chain; 18k 22k gold, fine silver, sterling silver; 1-1/2" long x 1-1/2" wide, 16" chain; 2005

Acknowledgements

I am truly fortunate to do what I love for a living. Without the endless support of my clan, this book would never have made it out of the idea stage.

Special thanks to Skyler for all the support and understanding, to Zelma, for the entrepreneurial inspiration and always believing in my artistic tendencies from an early age, to Chris... there isn't room to list all you have done (being my second pair of hands, my editor, my personal chef, and my perfect mate is a start). Finally to my students far and wide for asking so many great questions.

Victoria Lansford creates one-of-a-kind wearable pieces of art and art objects that recall the mystery and splendor of the ancient world, yet bring forth her own provocative vision. She has pushed the boundaries of design and execution in many old world techniques, including high relief Eastern repoussé, Russian filigree, chain making, and granulation throughout two decades of comprehensive exploration of metal as art.

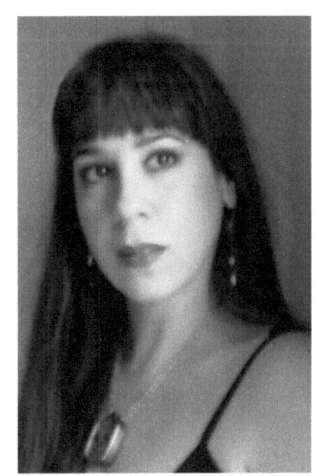

Victoria's award winning work has been featured in *Metalsmith* magazine's 2007 *Exhibition in Print,* multiple issues of *Lapidary Journal: Jewelry Artist* magazine, and *Art Jewelry* magazine, and on Home & Garden Television's 2007 season of *That's Clever.*

A long time educator in the arts, she is committed to sustaining ancient techniques through workshops and publications. Her instructional DVDs in the series, *Metal Techniques of Bronze Age Masters,* including *Russian Filigree* (2006) and *Rings* (2008), have sold throughout Europe, Asia, Australia and North and South America. Victoria's internationally collected artwork is available in art galleries throughout the U.S. and through her website, www.victorialansford.com. She lives in Atlanta, Georgia.